LIVING IN A WORLD
THAT CAN'T BE FIXED

ALSO BY CURTIS WHITE

NONFICTION

Monstrous Possibility: An Invitation to Literary Politics

The Middle Mind: Why Americans Don't Think for Themselves

The Spirit of Disobedience: Resisting the Charms of Fake Politics,
Mindless Consumption, and the Culture of Total Work

The Barbaric Heart: Faith, Money, and the Crisis of Nature

The Science Delusion: Asking the Big Questions
in Culture of Easy Answers

We, Robots: Staying Human in the Age of Big Data

FICTION

Heretical Songs

Metaphysics in the Midwest

The Idea of Home

Anarcho-Hindu

Memories of My Father Watching TV

Requiem

America's Magic Mountain

Lacking Character

LIVING IN A

WORLD

WORLD

THAT CAN'T BE FIXED

Reimagining
Counterculture
Today

CURTIS WHITE

Melville House
BROOKLYN   LONDON

LIVING IN A WORLD THAT CAN'T BE FIXED

First Melville House Printing: November 2019

Melville House Publishing
46 John Street
Brooklyn, NY 11201
and
Melville House UK
Suite 2000
16/18 Woodford Road
London E7 0HA

mhpbooks.com
@melvillehouse

ISBN: 978-1-61219-808-8
ISBN: 978-1-61219-809-5 (eBook)

Library of Congress Control Number: 2019945816

Designed by Alex Camlin

Printed in the United States of America
10 9 8 7 6 5 4 3 2 1

A catalog record for this book is available from the Library of Congress

"The counterculture, far more than merely 'meriting' attention, desperately requires it, since I am at a loss to know where, besides among these dissenting young people and their heirs of the next few generations, the radical discontent and innovation can be found that might transform this disoriented civilization of ours into something a human being can identify as home."

— Theodore Roszak, *The Making of a Counterculture*

Contents

Introduction . . . . *ix*

PART I. Living Out of Place *1*

PART II. What is Hidden in the Sun's Eye 23

PART III. Counterculture is Impertinent 37

PART IV. Counterculture is Improvisational 71

PART V. The Counter-counterculture 85

PART VI. Living in Place *109*

PART VII. *Coda* *121*

Acknowledgments. *135*

Endnotes. *137*

Introduction

This is a book about counterculture, and that's a problem. Counterculture is a word that is "fraught" with associations, connotations, and mendacities. The word counterculture has baggage, as we say ("freight" and "fraught" derive from the same Dutch root). Counterculture has been ridiculed for fifty years in the mainstream/corporate media as something that belongs only to the 1960s, to hedonist, weed-toking hippies, to communes, and to the failed social agenda of the high-'60s (no pun intended). But counterculture was not the creation of hippies, or of Beatniks, Dadaists, decadents, or the turn of the century Arts and Crafts movement before them. All of these movements were, however, countercultural in spirit, especially the Arts and Craft vision of a more authentic (more "handmade") form of living. (Coincidentally, I'm sitting on a Mission Oak sofa as I type this, Stickley chairs waiting around the kitchen table.) So, what was the source of the countercultural spirit they all shared?

Counterculture as we know it was a creation—or, better yet, an *improvisation*—of the English Romantics, the first artistic and social movement to knowingly and deliberately "drop out" of its own world. After the bloody disappointments of the French Revolution, they were no longer under the illusion that nations could be fixed—"what had been a pride / Was now a shame," as Wordsworth wrote—so instead of revolution the Romantics simply withdrew from the dominant culture of early 19th-century England. They dropped out of its rationalism, its industry, its obsession with business and trade, and, most personally, they dropped out of the English class system and its social hierarchies. All of the subsequent movements inspired by the Romantics shared their sense that the world they had been born into offered only punishingly narrow options for life. They felt, as Paul Goodman put it in the 1950s, that if they stayed within that world they had no choice except to "grow up absurd," diminished in their own eyes as human beings, and diminished morally for aiding the larger purposes of their world: poverty, oppression, and war. And so they improvised.

Our own moment is not without its absurdities and destructiveness. For instance, many young people now are offered the following: learn to work with intelligent machines, with computers and robots, or else. Never mind the conspicuous fact that to agree to that work not only has the effect of reducing themselves in their own eyes, but it makes them complicit with vast governmental and corporate structures that enforce inequality and have every appearance of being in the process of destroying the natural world. Well might a recent college graduate in one of the STEM disciplines complain, "It's not bad enough that we have to accept the absurdity of this work, this life as a data dog, but we have to aid and abet inequality and destruction while we're at it?!" As Goodman put it in *Growing Up Absurd* (2012), "The question is what it means to grow up into such a fact as: 'During my productive years I will spend eight hours a day doing what is no good.'"[1]

England's Romantic counterculture began with the "cult of feeling" that produced "weeping" novels like Henry Mackenzie's *The Man of Feeling* (1771). In Mackenzie's novel are prescient expressions of the Romantic such as, "There is a certain poetic ground, on which a man cannot tread without feelings that enlarge the heart: the causes of human depravity vanish before the romantic enthusiasm he professes . . ." Wordsworth, in his private world apart in the Lake District, turned Mackenzie's notion into the definition of poetry: "the spontaneous overflow of powerful feelings." Poetry created an alternative to a world dominated by "facts, facts, facts," as Thomas Gradgrind insisted in Charles Dickens's *Hard Times* (1854). (Dickens was himself famously weepy, and all of his heroes and heroines marked their virtues with tears.)

Later, the cult of feeling generated utopian ventures led by poets. Samuel Taylor Coleridge and Robert Southey planned to buy land in Pennsylvania for the purpose of creating a democratic commune called Pantisocracy where birth did not dictate social role, women were equal members, and art was the true if unacknowledged "legislator of the world," in Percy Bysshe Shelley's famous phrase. Shelley renounced his social station and estate (his grandfather was a Peer of the Realm) and devoted himself to poetry and then to atheism, nonviolence, vegetarianism, free love, and the emancipation of women. (Mary Shelley's mother was Mary Wollstonecraft, author of *A Vindication of the Rights of Woman* (1792), one of the founding texts of feminism.)

Romanticism was not merely a period in art history; it was a social movement first. It was a rebellion against a rigid class system that condemned individuals to specific and limited social roles and denied their individual genius, leaving graveyards full of unrealized "human potential," as we'd say, or "mute inglorious Miltons," as Thomas Gray put it in his "Elegy Written in a Country Churchyard" (1751). The "Elegy" prefigured the class resentments that would define the English Romantics, and for which upper-class critics attacked them. In particular, Keats was crudely criticized for being of the Cockney School of poetry, a vicious dig at his working class birth. But Keats's critics understood something that was not obvious: this new breed of poet was a threat to their status and their interests.

There is a remarkable pattern in the biographies of the English Romantics: all rebelled against the plans that England had for them. Coleridge was meant to be a clergyman, Keats a surgeon, and Shelley a Peer. Wordsworth looked in horror upon the prospect of "vegetating on a paltry curacy." What England offered was too limited, and the Romantics wanted something "oceanic," something "with the feeling of the eternal," as the French novelist Romain Rolland expressed it in a letter to a skeptical Sigmund Freud.* So they refused their "station in life." They wanted to be Poets with a capital P. But Poet was not an approved role available to anybody, rich or poor. To say, "I want to be a poet," was much like the young troubadour of the present saying, "I don't want to write code for Google. I want to write songs and play in a band." To be a poet was in essence to say "fuck off" to everything about the world at that point—the monarchs, the nobility, the men of business, the endless wars, and the gross inequality. The Romantics were war dodgers,

. . . .

*   See Caspar David Friedrich's oil painting *Wanderer Above the Sea of Fog* (1818) for an image of the oceanic.

blasphemers, and communalists, which is why they lived in fear of prison under the "Sedition and Blasphemy" laws that the Tories established after the French Revolution as a means of controlling revolutionaries, pamphleteers, atheists, and poets. (A spy was assigned to observe the young radicals Wordsworth and Coleridge. This spy reported that the two were suspiciously interested in "spy nozy," also known as Spinoza.)

This hatred for the class system has never ceased to animate some of England's best poets and writers. For instance, the novelist Paul Scott in his brilliant *Raj Quartet* (1965–1975) writes this, referring to the English administrators of the British Raj in colonial India:

> They were predictable people, predictable because they worked for the robot. What the robot said they would also say, what the robot did they would do, and what the robot believed was what they believed because people like them had fed that belief into it. And they would always be right so long as the robot worked, because the robot was the standard of rightness.
>
> There was no *originating passion* in them. Whatever they felt that was original would die the moment it came into conflict with what the robot was geared to feel.

Domination by the great robot (the duties of imperial England's class system)? Originating passion (Wordsworth's "feeling")? Readers might respond positively or negatively to this passage, but they would be unlikely to say, "Ah, Romanticism is alive!" But that is exactly what this passage says: the spirit of Romanticism lives.

That's a long way of saying that I will not limit my use of the term "counterculture" to the 1960s. I will use the term to indicate a social movement more than two centuries old whose fundamental purpose has been to displace the violence and inequality of Western capitalist culture. That's its "idea," even if every particular counter-cultural instance of that idea has been limited or flawed, and many of its participants have been crazy or clueless. And yet many of us now feel a deep gratitude to this tradition, especially to its recent Anglo-American variation.

I grew up in a prefab East Bay suburb in the 1950s (speaking of passionless robots), a place where uncomprehending alienation was the world and the world was a lusterless fate. But I was fortunate to live near San Francisco and the music culture of the late '60s. Simply put, hippy culture, psychedelia, and anti-war dissidence called to me and I ran, laughing, to embrace it all. I may have thought that I was joining hippy culture, but in fact I was throwing the weight of my young being behind the Romantic appeal of "originating passion."

Just as relevant, in the summer of 1969, the summer before my freshman year at the University of San Francisco, I joined a group of Marxist autodidacts in a rented office space in downtown Hayward and, using materials from the Quaker's American Friends Service Committee, studied to become a draft counselor. But in that office were magazines—*Ramparts, The Berkeley Barb, The San Francisco Oracle, National Lampoon*—and pamphlets analyzing the United States's motives for the war in Vietnam, the role of money and militarism, and revealing the facts about what our "boots on the ground" meant to the people of Vietnam and to our own soldiers.

I was very surprised by all this. I'd never seen anything like it. It certainly wasn't the sort of stuff I was offered in high school. But I reached a quick conclusion: "Oh," I thought, "this is what it's like to think. This is what honesty feels like. Somebody is bothering to tell me the truth." I'd never felt so alive before—not one of the living dead, not another creature of my culture, not another one of Paul Scott's robots.

As a consequence, I became deeply skeptical of loyalty to a nation that asked its young to risk their lives in corrupt wars, and I was skeptical that I could be loyal to a social system that offered such one-dimensional lives to its children. But radical honesty? Now, *that* I could be loyal to. The music I heard at the Fillmore Auditorium, *that* I could be loyal to. Intelligence, honesty, and music opened things up for me, and created what the first hippies, the Haight-Ashbury's communal anarchists the Diggers, called "free frame of reference." I was free in my mind to join with others in the creation of a world as much unlike the one we knew as possible.

I say I became skeptical, but that's not quite right. Skepticism has negative connotations suggesting a degree of cynicism, but I was not and am not cynical. What I learned in that Hayward office space was how to "read against the grain," how, in this context, to resist the assumption that my country would not lie to me and must be telling the truth. Reading against the grain is not about being skeptical. Reading against the grain is about *transformation*. Debunking the truth claims of social authorities (whether state, community, or family) opens the way to creating alternatives (better ways to think, better ways to live).

I would go on to more sophisticated versions of this experience as a university student, reading more of the intellectual heroes of the era, Marcuse, Roszak, Sartre, the anti-psychologist R. D. Laing, and eventually Marx and the pantheon of Western Marxist intellectuals, especially Theodor Adorno. But I had learned something in that grim little office in Hayward that I couldn't have learned elsewhere, not even through Adorno. I learned that this critical intelligence, this truth-telling, this honesty, does not happen in the big world, in what I would learn to call the "dominant culture"; it happens in spaces set apart and inhabited by "freaks" and political radicals, demographics that seemed happily inexhaustible in the Bay Area in 1969. In other words, my political and personal enlightenment came among people who had dropped out of the world as we'd known it. What Allen Ginsberg called the Two Tribes—Berkeley politicos and San Francisco hippies—were united in me and many others. Berkeley's socialists provided a critique of what we endured, and San Francisco's counterculture provided an alternative.

In my sixty-eight years on the planet, the only political thought that I have seen succeed to any degree in creating conditions where intelligence, mutual caring, beauty, and health counted for more than power and profit has not been socialism, or communism, or democracy, and certainly not capitalism. It has been counterculture.

Counterculture is civil disobedience as a way of life.

But the point of this book is not to look back. Of course, it's useful to know that we have a distinguished tradition to appeal to, a lineage, but that's finally not the point. The point is to recognize that counterculture and its refusal to join the world in bloody progress is still a viable option. For us. Now. And that is in spite of the wellheeled efforts of Democrats and Republicans alike along with their handmaids in the corporate media to tell us that counterculture is not an option, that it is a failure, a dead thing. For me, the point is to use the traditions of counterculture *to create strategies for living in a world that can't be fixed.*

This book is intended not only as a call to countercultural arms, as if we were to say, "Citizens of the world . . . relax!" It is also intended as something that seeks the freedom, the playfulness, the intelligence, and the honesty of counterculture. In this book I try to write in counterculture's creative aura.

So, a few important understandings before setting off. Although there is a logic to this book, it is as much a "performance" as an "argument." The argument begins with an account of the problem (Parts I and II): all of the millions of people on this planet who lack a sense of *place*, a sense of belonging to a place that they know as their home; and all of the millions of people who live in isolation—whether that means living under a freeway overpass or 24/7 in front of a smartphone—who experience firsthand our current epidemic of mass loneliness, depression, drug abuse, and suicide.

In response to this problem are two sections (Parts III and IV) that describe counterculture as both a critique and an alternative way of living. Counterculture, I contend, is both *impertinent* and *improvisational.* Counterculture lives through a thoughtful and often comic scorn for the status quo. It makes itself impertinent, both insolent and useless to the purposes of the larger world. Released by this impertinence from the burden of what others take to be "reality," counterculture proceeds to improvise an alternative. As the hippies put it, counterculture "does its own thing." It improvises a counter-world. In this way, it seeks both freedom and happiness. *What about God?*

My argument continues with a sort of reprise, da capo, of the problem, emphasizing the ways in which the dominant culture frustrates or prohibits counterculture (Part V), followed by two concluding sections (Parts VI and VII) in which I consider what counterculture can mean for us now. That's the logic of this book, but not its entirety.

If the world cannot be fixed, it is because the institutions that are charged with fixing it are actively doing the opposite, are energetically treating the world not as the subject of care but as the object of self-enrichment and self-aggrandizement. I do not hope for the Democratic Party or even the Democratic Socialists to fix this situation. As Nancy Pelosi remarked at a CNN town hall meeting in 2018: "We're all capitalists, and that's the way it is." Even Elizabeth Warren has confessed that "I believe in markets." To both of them we ought to reply, impertinently, "So much the worse for your world, representatives! You leave us no choice except to make our own." We must be *impertinent* in order not to do what the robots (among whom we must include Speaker Pelosi) want us to do. In addition, we will need to re-learn the power of *improvisation* in order to create worlds that we might choose to live in, might be happy to live in, as opposed to the world that we do live in, the one that is administered by our masters.

This may not sound like something you know how to do, and in truth nobody does. It is mostly a world to be discovered. But because of the threat of climate disaster and nuclear war, things out of all proportion to anything our species has ever experienced, we will need to figure it out. As Taj Mahal sang in 1969, "You're gonna need somebody on your bond." You're gonna need other people if you want to get to heaven, or for us, forget heaven, we're gonna need other bodies on our bond just to survive. We may not need a socialist state, but we will need social bonds—neighbors or comrades, community or congregation, doesn't matter what you call them—if we are to survive the calamities that threaten us.

This renewed social bonding is, obviously, not what is happening now. Millions of jobs have been added to urban areas since the Great Recession, but many of the people in those jobs live in expensive apartment ghettos where employees are warehoused in human abstraction. It's hard to imagine what those mostly young people will do at the "end of civilization" that some climate scientists are predicting for us.

In other words, there is an element not only of socialism but of survivalism, a socialist survivalism, if you will, in the countercultures we will create. Counterculture provides a way forward. While working through it, we no longer soak in puddles of anxiety waiting for Rachel Maddow to explain it all to us, or wait for the House of Representatives to get busy and impeach somebody, anybody, to "lock them up!" Instead we will be living, and *enlarging.* Not waiting for the revolution and the arrival of the perfected socialist state or even an imperfect version thereof (which is certainly what we'd get), but living now in our own strength and creativity.

That is what I'd like to persuade my readers of, but I will often seek to persuade in the way that music persuades: by providing an experience that readers will want to join and carry forward. This book is theatrical as well as discursive, especially in its three "improvisations," tucked in among the arguments: my guitar solos, so to speak. In other words, this book is a performance intended as an example of a possible intellectual/literary counterculture. And that's important because in these improvisations the book tries to be what it calls for.

Finally, this is not a how-to book. I am not trying to persuade anybody to do anything in particular, and I'm certainly not trying to give instructions for making a chicken coop. Like Nietzsche's *Human, All Too Human*, this is a book seeking companions, seeking "free spirits." In a sense, I'm trying not only to persuade but to *seduce*, seduce into the awareness that this or something like this is what we WANT—in both senses of the term: what we lack and what we desire.

Theodor Adorno famously said that in capitalist culture "Life does not live." So, let's live. But live how? It is in the nature of counterculture to refuse the world as something already determined. It creates a welcoming openness to change, to drift, to try things. It is laughing freedom. It is disenchanted with capitalist reality and says, "Dissolve! Diffuse! Dissipate! In order to recreate!" (Coleridge).

That's the neighborhood I want to live in!

Meet the new boss

Same as the old boss

PART
I
Whining

LIVING OUT OF PLACE

Human cultures are about *place*: where to live, and *home*: how to live and with whom. In Western capitalist culture, home is where the money is. And place, increasingly, is an abstraction. Our sense of place becomes more abstract, and scattered to the virtual winds, with each ever-more-advanced smart gizmo that we plug in our ears, strap to our wrists, and, with the innovations of the smart home, sleep in, securely we imagine. Come the day when these abstractions fail—the collapse of the financial system, or the energy infrastructure, or the failure of the climate itself—we will realize that we were in truth always out of place and homeless.

Perhaps this is why the plight of refugees has such grim fascination for us: there but for fate go we. The homeless and placeless—whether on a raft off the Greek coastline or in an RV in Seattle—make us anxious, but we don't seem to be able to say quite *why* they make us anxious. We haven't got any skin in that game . . . have we? In the fall of 2017 two feature-length documentaries by prominent artists—Ai Weiwei and Agnès Varda—took up the challenge of thinking about people out of place with very different results.

Ai Weiwei's 2017 documentary *Human Flow* is an unrelenting visualization of the movement of refugees in all parts of the global south, people dispersed by war, poverty, and climate change, from

Syria to Myanmar to Africa and to Mexico. It is about people out of place. It is a visually sobering film and does much to humanize their otherwise abstract sorrows. But it is curiously unlike most documentaries of its kind because it is not diagnostic. Ai Weiwei is not interested in analyzing why this "flow" is happening, and he does not prescribe any sort of remedy. Perhaps, given his own history as a refugee from Chinese communist oppression, a Marxist critique of global capital and its colonialist past is an awkward fit for him. (Not that there is anything remotely Marxist about China.) In any case, no such analysis is offered. Weiwei is no Zola, and he utters no "j'accuse."

The closest he comes to something like an ideological judgment is a vaguely eighteenth-century appeal to "humanity," as in our "shared humanity," which becomes the reason that we "should not ignore" the plight of people we ought to "care for," and that, he emphasizes repeatedly, we ought to "respect." In this way he joins Pope Francis in lamenting the "indifference of the world."

Weiwei's humanitarian concern is given voice by disconsolate officials of the United Nations and various NGOs who condemn the indifference of someone—the West, the World, You the Privileged Viewer?—but their complaints are like the keening and ululating of professional mourners. In the end, they are merely the paternalistic lamentations of the culprits, and are often seen in that light by the people that the officials claim to be helping.

As activist Masoud Qahar describes the situation at the Elliniko refugee camp in Greece:

> Some NGOs are coming to help, but it's just for two or three days. They play with kids, take a lot of pictures of the kids, and

they take money for this. A lot of news channels come here and make movies, documentaries. They have a business [profiting from] the refugees. [It's] like a zoo, and we're like animals [to the NGOs and media].²

Or, as Tessa Quayle, the leftist hero of John le Carré's *The Constant Gardener* (2001), observes, when she hears the "managerial elite" appealing to "Humanity, Altruism, Duty to Mankind, I want to vomit." Put more diplomatically, as Peter Buffett has in the opinion pages of *The New York Times*, "[Philanthropists] are searching for answers with their right hand to problems that others in the room have created with their left." This is most obviously true when the refugees are fleeing the consequences of climate change, whether African droughts, sinking Pacific islands, or rising North American shorelines. First World philanthropy is, in Buffett's telling phrase, "conscience laundering."³ Weiwei is tone deaf to this irony, and his film is precious close to being part of this institutional laundromat.

What Weiwei does explore fully is the novel vision of these fantastic migrations. *Human Flow* is a perversely beautiful movie, with many giddy overheads taken from drones of tent camps, boats, massive piles of abandoned life jackets, and lines of trekking asylum seekers. The film feels closer to *National Geographic* photography of vast herds of zebras migrating in the Serengeti than to, say, the gritty intimacy of Alain Resnais's documentary on the Holocaust, *Night and Fog* (1956).

To put it bluntly, *Human Flow* aestheticizes the refugee crisis. Perhaps this is inevitable. Why else see a movie about refugees made by Weiwei? Part of the attraction of the movie is, of course, the fact that it was made by an artist famous for creating confrontational public art. But in this case the confrontation is meaningless because it doesn't know what to ask for. It is protest without purpose. Even so, the question should not be "does he aestheticize suffering?" as if aestheticizing were always the wrong thing to do. The question should be "does the aestheticizing lead to or at least suggest a way forward?" Does it offer ideology (the mere consumption of aesthetic pleasure bought and paid for) or does it offer utopia (the rejection of the world as it stands and the offer of an alternative)? Crudely, is it *National Geographic* or Jean-Luc Godard?

Or Agnès Varda.   *Never news of film*

In the same season that *Human Flow* was making the rounds of art house theaters in the United States, the great French *Nouvelle Vague* filmmaker Agnès Varda was collaborating with the artist JR on *Faces Places (Visages, Villages)*. In the film, Varda and JR (like Weiwei, an installation artist) travel rural France meeting with waitresses, mailmen, miners, and factory workers, and photographing them in JR's mobile photo booth. These portraits are then enlarged and pasted to the buildings that they work and live in—barns, abandoned homes, shipping containers—creating dramatic pop-up artworks.

As with *Human Flow*, *Faces Places* is disarmingly non-ideological, although there is every opportunity for making familiar political judgments. Everyone seems involved in one social ill or another: pollution, industrial farming, cruelty to animals, global shipping of consumer goods, etc., but the filmmakers do not hold the people responsible for the economic mechanisms within which they have no choice except to work. Rather, the people and, to a degree, the economic mechanisms are accepted as they are. They are real. The central metaphor, here, is "seeing": both seeing "what is" without judgment, and seeing "what is" transformed through art.

Unlike Weiwei's distanced call for "respect," Varda and JR immerse themselves in the places they discover. They enact compassion and solidarity. They are one with their subjects. This compassion begins with the relationship between the two artists. Varda is aging, frail, and losing her eyesight.* JR treats Varda as the Buddha would, as if she were his mother. Together JR and Varda treat every human they encounter as if they were their mother. The people they meet are not treated as a spectacle but as a gathering, a family affair.

Nevertheless, *Faces Places* is politically radical because, unlike *Human Flow*, its understated protest does ask for something. For the moment in which JR's art installations exist, before the next rain dissolves the glue and removes the image, we are allowed to imagine that the people own their built environments, whether factory or village, rather than the reverse. When the film's subjects see themselves superimposed on abandoned brick miners' homes, factory walls, and shipping containers, they feel some vanity, but their larger feeling is triumph. They are no longer the victims of an economic mechanism beyond their understanding; rather, they are its creators, never mind what the bank and the political state claim. The corporate state cannot determine economic and social relations through command alone; the people themselves must reproduce both work and social relations day by day. What Varda and JR show is that *the people are already in control*, they just don't know it. The filmmakers proceed as if the boss doesn't exist, and the people are, therefore, free.

This point is brought home poignantly when Varda and JR set

* *

*   Varda died in early 2019.

up shop with local residents at a failed housing project. Squatters for a day, they occupy the shells of these homes as if they were playhouses, sharing food and pasting up photographs of themselves in remembrance of a lost world, and in rehearsal for a world to come. In essence, they rediscover the Commons, the world prior to private property's great enclosure of the land. This picnic among the ruins of private property is the film's most joyful moment. They look like squatters, but they're really natives who have returned to claim their ancestral home . . . returned to claim their *place*.

This scene offers a further pleasure: the audience's happy recognition that *this is the way the world ought to be*. Human is reconciled to human, to work, and to animals (especially goats!). In accomplishing this, the artwork provides a way forward. *Faces Places* is art *engagée*, as Sartre put it. Its pleasures are transformational. It creates a powerful sense of the Ought, without which no revolution can begin. It creates a powerful sense of the Demand, without which no revolution can move forward. As Slavoj Žižek writes, "Every historical situation contains its own unique utopian perspective, an immanent vision of what is wrong with it, an ideal representation of how, with some changes, the situation could be rendered much better."4

That is Varda and JR's gift to us: a story about the authentic relationship of people to their world, a profound as-if. Our challenge is to live *as if* this relationship were real *now*, and not in some uncertain future. That is the process through which the work of art creates its own appropriate world. The "otherness" of the work of art is both critique (of what we have) and solution (an act that does not merely appeal to but that *is* the world we want).

Seen in this way, *Faces Places* is not a film about how art helps one thing or another, or about how art is a complement to real political activity. You know, a little music or a poem after the march and after the heavy hitters have made their speeches. Art is not something that requires the more serious intervention of a political movement in order to achieve its ends. Rather, art destroys the world as it is and replaces it with something that is utterly other. (Thus the superimposition of the faces of workers on shipping containers, the human suddenly and impossibly larger than the industrial.) As art has done since the Romantics, *Faces Places* demands something other than the dictatorship of the present. It is an incitement to change. It is the vigorous call for what John Kenneth Galbraith called a "countervailing power." It is a call for counterculture.

The work of art is not an ornament; it is where the artist thinks you should want to live, because the world it suggests is more intelligent, or more ruthlessly true, or more beautiful, or all of the above.

If Varda and JR's film provides us with an instance of art's political potential, it also shows how powerless and impoverished we are at present. It shows how far we have to go and how difficult the way will be. Midway through the film, they meet a homeless man—old, thin, shoulder-length dreads, nearly toothless—who offers to show them his home. It is a little den hidden in thickets where he has created a refuge of found objects and fanciful, colorful carvings, whirligigs, festoons, and childish improvisations. It is the "objective correlative" of his inner life, which is unexpectedly happy.

The moment is cognitively dissonant. Few of us would wish to trade places with him; in fact, many of us would feel that we need to be protected from him. The homeless produce a complex fear in us. The homeless frighten us both directly (disgust, fear of violence) and indirectly (you could become one of them if you don't stay in line, keep your job, pay your debts). Yet, in this instance, missing teeth be damned, there is something deeply appealing about this man's fanciful home—something free, and full of the happiness of human play. After we see his hideaway, he is transformed into something that is not threatening at all, but . . . perhaps "lovable" is the appropriate word. Can he and his little world apart be *desirable*? Unlike the disconsolate immigrants of *Human Flow*, this man is in place. He is *at home* in a world of his making.

Is this beggar's little paradise a sad delusion? Is it an image of the impotence of art to achieve the world it wants? An image of art's defeat? Of Varda and JR's defeat? Of human defeat? Or do its details show not that we are defeated, but how far we have to go? It is a sign, in spite of everything, of what we must do: transcend the world as it is through acts of self-creation.

IMPROVISATION: H+1

Ai Weiwei is no Varda and certainly no Lenin. If there is a diagnosis to be made for why this "human flow" is happening or "what's to be done," he leaves it to someone else. The obvious case to be made, so well made by Slavoj Žižek, is that these human migrations are the consequence of capitalism's ongoing looting of the land and the people of the Global South. These places have "dropped out of history." They are inhabited only by the "unneeded," the expendable, lumpen populations from failed states, the states themselves like "the blank spaces in ancient maps," terra incognita as far as the

First World is concerned. In short, from a First World point of view, the suffering of refugees is their own doing, and the victims are to blame. They are hopeless, terminal cases for which there are limits on what can be done, respect or no respect, shared humanity or no.

The way that *Human Flow* visualizes the migration of refugees, from the very idea that they constitute a "flow" (as if Weiwei were considering the lava pouring from the Kilauea volcano in the spring of 2018) to the way it borrows filmic techniques from a very familiar sort of nature photography, led me to try to imagine the cause of this "humanitarian disaster" (in the trivializing lingo of the United Nations) in naturalistic rather than political-economic terms. I wondered, "Why are these animals behaving in this way?" After all, in the Anthropocene we're not the only living things seeking new homes, as warm water fish push into the Arctic and trees colonize ground once held by glaciers.

The philosopher Alain Badiou argues that humans are a "slightly sad animal" that "aspires to enjoyment." The human animal's hopes are not abstract and not something for a manifesto. As with any animal, what humans aspire to is, to use a clinical term, the pleasure of homeostasis. What we all want, refugees included, is the maintenance of the pleasure of being well—warm, fed, companionable, outward looking, and safe.

The human animal's hopes are in its body. It is this that makes the lives of refugees and the homeless seem so hopeless, caught as they are in "bare life" (Giorgio Agamben), a state in which humans are reduced to their bodies, as if the body were already a sort of corpse, deprived of all rights and resources.

But to think that the rootless animal that we see in *Human Flow*, forced out of its first home, futilely moving from place to place, often for reasons that are no more than rumors about how welcoming a certain place might be, to think that this animal is only after what will minimally suffice is to grossly misunderstand it. It obviously wants more than bare life, otherwise it would simply sit wherever it finds itself and suffer, but it also wants something more than a friendly welcome, a cup of tea, a meal, and other comforts of homeostasis offered by refugee camps.

What better describes this animal's reality is something more like N+1. I am not referring to the N+1 of physics, about which I know nothing, but to the N+1 of cycling, where the number of bikes one can own is determined by the number of bikes one already owns +1. Say I own three bikes and I can ride on any of them at any time to my heart and legs' content. Surely, I should be in bicycle homeostasis. I should even be bicycle homeo-ecstatic. But it seems that that stasis can always be supplemented, indefinitely if not infinitely, through the addition of new bikes. For example, Robin Williams owned over a hundred bikes, eighty-seven of which were auctioned after his death. Of course, this idea isn't limited to bikes: Tom Hanks owns one hundred typewriters and is reportedly holding firm at that number (unless that 1906 Royal Standard 1 comes on the market?). And a real showstopper, Jay Leno owns 169 cars (including a Stanley Steamer), 117 motorcycles, and one really big garage (star of the television program "Jay Leno's Garage").

This, obviously, is not a description of homeostasis. It is homeostasis plus, or H+1, and it is not a pathology of the super-rich, it is our native condition. It is the political economy of our biology. Although 98.6°F is our baseline body temperature, we are better understood as the warm-blooded mammal that thinks it could always be a little warmer. Or, as lifestyle entrepreneur Suze Yalof

Schwartz has announced revealingly on her website Tall Skinny Rich, "Everyone can look a little taller, skinnier, richer."

This principle holds true most obviously for the oligarchs among us, the uppermost one percent who would seem to have saturated this +1. But, as my Hollywood examples show, that's not how they feel about it. And while we're wondering, "What's wrong with them? Why are they so greedy?" we should also acknowledge that we're not as unlike them as we might imagine. We're also clicking on PayPal, or pushing our Working Assets Better World MasterCard toward the clerk who is happily ringing up our next bicycle, laptop, or eyeliner.

As Julie Creswell explains in the Business section of *The New York Times*:

> Young shoppers are the driving force behind a boom in the cosmetics industry. Always camera ready, they are buying and using almost 25 percent more cosmetics than they did just two years ago and significantly more than baby boomers, according to the research firm NPD. And millennials who identify themselves as "makeup enthusiasts," NPD found, are using six products each day. "[Makeup is] popular among millennials because it looks great in a selfie,"* said Ms. Hertzmark Hudis, group president at Estée Lauder.[5]

Even the disembodied online gamers, those hearty if virtual souls, feel they must add always one more "in-game extra" through endless "microtransactions" that purchase, say, a superior "Darth Vader choke hold," guaranteed to give the buyer a tactical advantage in the next

. . . .

* The idea that "makeup is popular because it looks great in a selfie" belongs in the Museum of Tautological Marvels.

round of online wargasm. Of course, the sorrows of the young and hyperreal are well known and need no rehearsing here. It is enough to observe how completely they understand the consumer materialist's saving conviction: "The winner is the one with the most toys."

Or, let's be honest, the most toys +1.*

Revealingly, the rich are not indifferent to our complaints about their accumulation of cars, boats, homes, bicycles, typewriters, and eyeliner. Quite to the contrary, the rich feel what anyone feels when criticized: threatened. Our complaints about their "greed" is threatening not to their greediness, because they have no intention of willingly changing, but to their sense of homeostatic well-being. The oligarch's primary anxiety is not that he has some sort of addiction to the accumulation of things, especially that money thing; his primary anxiety is that he might be diminished. Once life becomes a matter of diminution, of H-1, there is no knowing where it stops. The oligarch starts to feel like the Wicked Witch of the West: "I'm melting!" That feeling, in turn, makes him think that there is now another reason for +1: self-preservation and security. Survival! Sure, some of them might own eighty-seven bikes, or, like Paul Manafort, five houses in five of the world's most opulent destinations, or five yachts moored in five of the world's most exotic harbors, but the idea that there are people who would like to take one or more of those things away frightens them.

. . . .

* I don't mean to limit H+1 to material things. There is also an H+1 of the psyche: You can always get a little more recognition for being a writer or an athlete or whatever it is that you organize your identity around—more awards, more fame, more friends, more likes, more followers on Twitter. Without the personal recognition offered by fans, institutions, money, and things, we fear that we may not exist at all.

Even oligarchs are human animals (all-too-human, as Nietzsche might say of them) and sweetly reason, "My dear friends and family and brothers on the Street [as in Wall Street] own homes and cars and bikes, too, so I will stand shoulder to shoulder with them. 'They're good guys!' as President Trump says. While I'm at it, I'd better buy two more bikes so that if they do take away a few bikes I'll still have my eighty-seven." But wait just a few months and the eighty-nine bikes become the new "normal," the new "H," which is now the object of renewed threat from "losers" (as Trump likes to call anyone lacking a billionaire's resources and bicycles) who "envy my hard work and success." In spite of every appearance, as if they were refugees plotting their way across the Mediterranean Sea with their last possessions in duffle bags on their backs, they are *afraid*. As Antonio Negri and Michael Hardt write in *Assembly*: "Scratch the surface of private property's veneer of security and you will find its real foundation: fear."[6]

The 2017 Republican re-writing of the tax code is an instance of this psychology. For the super-rich, there is no question of *needing* more money. There is only the question of protecting what is for them minimal, or homeostatic. In the weaponized language of the Left, they may be "privileged" and "entitled," but that's not how they see it. They have every intention of protecting what they feel are necessities. The Great Recession of 2008 was a trauma, but how bad will the next one be? And so they take Iago's advice for Roderigo to "put money in thy purse." Not to take advantage of the opportunity that this tax giveaway offers is to make themselves feel anxious and vulnerable, in other words, not safe. They don't want to regret, somewhere down the economic road, that "we should have taken that money while we could. And now look at us!"

Not to take advantage of the opportunity is also to feel that they are not part of their community, the one percent, the "right people," the "successful," to use Trump's lingo again. Some Republican senators may have their spats with Trump, but when it comes time to vote for a tax break for the rich they will *vote their conscience*: and their conscience, such as it is, is largely a matter of family fealty. This fealty is especially strong if, as with Utah's Senator Orrin Hatch, the upper class was originally aspirational, something one looked toward longingly, and now that one is a member, it's all about "solidarity forever." Ask the old guys and gals on the first tee at Mar-a-Lago. Such behavior among the most intensely rich is not about greed or even pleasure: it is about the fear of being returned to an a-homeostatic, or heterostatic, condition in which they become, in their shared mind, among the dispossessed of the earth, even if that means only dispossessed of a high-end bicycle, car, home, or swank hotel.

This is the sort of argument that is made not by greedy or otherwise ethically deficient people. It is the sort of argument that the bodies of animals make, impoverished refugees included. One might think that the only thing that the tens of thousands of desperate people in *Human Flow* want is simply a livable minimum, something not so far on the other side of "bare life": shelter, food, safety, and the respect of someone like Ai Weiwei, whatever that's worth. But in a revealing scene, an adolescent girl at the Tempelhof Airport refugee camp in Germany has a complaint: in spite of the cleanliness, the ready availability of nourishing food, and the safety, she's bored! For her, a bicycle would be nice indeed.

She's all in with H+1.

But who stops with a bicycle? A car when she turns sixteen? A small palette of eye shadow for selfies? A smartphone for taking the selfie? A rich husband attracted by the selfie? A little vacation cottage on one of those nice Greek islands she saw from the lifeboat that brought her over from Turkey? Not to desire in this way betrays not only the body, it also betrays the community of teenage girls she imagines herself to be part of, all of whom are on record as bored and in need of a bicycle for now, a car later, cosmetics for sure later on, and that smartphone, if her parents would just stop being losers and get with the program. In other words, *what biology asserts, socialization assures*—socialization *normalizes* behavior that is in fact self-destructive.

Again, this is not the argument of a greedy person. This is the sort of argument that the bodies of animals make. Consider the fat person who has decided to lose some weight. He goes on a diet, exercises, and quickly loses ten or twenty pounds, at which point his body, still thirty pounds overweight and well on its way to an unhappy encounter with diabetes, decides that it is being starved. So it starts to shut down his metabolism and begins to whine in that incontestable way that fat cells have, like something between the pleading of a hungry baby and the shrieking of a monkey. A certain weird, if familiar, moral panic sets in, driven by both the bad and better angels of his nature: "Feed me, for God's sake! I'm being deprived of a basic human right! *Steak au poivre*! Chocolate mousse! Oh well, maybe if I stay on the diet, Oprah will give me a car."

In an odd way, this is why Nietzsche was right to say that we are the psychological animal, because we are forever in the process of explaining to ourselves the motivation for, the *reason* behind, our animal behavior, even when that behavior is simply the whining of fat cells. It is also why Nietzsche was right to think that moral condemnation—*"they're greedy!"*—is an inadequate way of thinking about what kind of animal we are.

Do these "animal facts" excuse the First World's role in causing the misery of refugees of the Global South? Does it mean "we'd all do what the oligarchs do, given the chance"? No. What it means is that there is something starkly lacking in the way we ordinarily talk about the immiseration of entire human populations, and lacking about the way we consider those lucky humans who observe them from a condition of rarified comfort.

It is not useful to frame the problem solely in terms of greed and indifference because there's a sense in which we are a "greedy" animal, an animal that lives in a certain kind of want, or desire. Generally, we all desire happiness, however that is understood, and apparently it is not easily understood, or attained, but certainly no one is to be blamed for seeking it. Happiness arrives when we feel free to live in curiosity and confidence in human community. H+I is at its best when it is the dance of self-creation. *That* is what Varda and JR reveal so beautifully. The problem comes when H+I is distorted, when we think that only our own +I matters and that having to live equitably with others is an intolerable limit on our individual projects. H+I is a poison when it is only about Me.

So the problem is not our sinfulness, the problem is that whether migrant, oligarch, or something in the more or less habitable middle, we are profoundly dislocated and disconnected from each other. We are *all* out of place, and because of that we suffer through a sort of universal unease. You'd think that we'd want to remedy that; we're social animals, after all. Yet, tragically, we're more likely to believe that keeping others at a distance works to our advantage. Keep the homeless, the dirty, all those people in boats and rafts, the long lines of trekkers in the desert, the climate refugees, the rent refugees and other losers, the masses piled up against one national border or another, one "big beautiful wall," keep them all away. We do this because when people are at a distance—even if that just means in a not-so-faraway opiate hovel in central Ohio—we can treat them as mostly unreal things to which we owe very little.

For an extreme example, the Saudis murdered and starved tens of thousands of Yemenis by employing weapons that we sold to them and trained them to use, and President Trump excused the butchery by saying that our economy, and thus our happiness, needed the billions the Saudis were paying us for the weapons. The people of Yemen became part of a calculus of private benefit in which H+I expressed itself in monstrously destructive terms. We behaved like pseudo-adults chasing happiness with a slide rule (or an algorithm), a condition more dangerous than a child with a gun. But making people part of a calculus of private benefit does not work to our advantage at all, as this dying world is trying to tell us.

Whether we are on a raft or a yacht, we are all *dis-placed*. Weiwei feels this distance between us, as he shows in what is either the low point of the film or the moment of its greatest honesty. Weiwei is talking to a refugee, exchanging passports, joking good-naturedly, when he says, "I respect you."

> Refugee: We have to respect you.
> Ai Weiwei: I respect your passport, and I respect you.

But surely the audience should be wondering, "Ai Weiwei, of what earthly good is your respect?" And "have to"? Is the nameless refugee bitter about his servile obligation? Is he another Caliban? Will he soon say, "You taught me language: and my profit on't / Is, I know how to curse . . ."? Certainly some among the immigrant communities of Paris and Cologne and the Molenbeek neighborhood of Brussels have learned to curse. Will the refugee in this scene soon join them? The scene is one of dis-ease, not mutual recognition, not solidarity. It is about isolation and about the gap between the two men: the refugee doesn't know where he is going, while Weiwei is fully aware that he will return to Berlin and the life of an international art celebrity. *Human Flow* has no idea how to heal that gap, that wound, but at least the film acknowledges it, however awkwardly.

By contrast, the last images in *Faces Places* is of an old and failing woman, Varda herself, "Waiting for Godard" (Jean-Luc Godard, who has failed to show for the film's final scene), dragging a tiny overnight bag behind her as if it were her last possession, merely one of the miserably mobile of the world. She is in solidarity with her subjects—waitresses, workers, the homeless—in a way that Ai Weiwei is not, a solidarity she expresses through her own human failing. JR's art installations serve to make other people real, not abstractions, not hallucinations floating on the horizon that we wish would float a little farther still so that they couldn't be seen at all. Once they are real for us, our feelings about them change. We cannot be "indifferent." They become the focus of our caring, just as Varda shows us in encounter after encounter. Unlike Weiwei, who is often content to see refugees from a cinematic distance, Varda is always bringing people *closer* to her. This is the work of art's "sympathetic imagination"—learning what it is like to be other people.* It has been a large part of the revolution begun by the Romantics ever since Wordsworth wrote "Resolution and Independence," a poem in which the poet meets an old man, a leech picker, in whom he discovers, to his surprise, an enlightened mind:

> *I could have laughed myself to scorn to find*
> *In that decrepit Man so firm a mind.*

In this remarkable moment, Wordsworth creates a little community of caring, or, perhaps, it could be called a church. As Christianity puts it, "Where three are, there is the Church" (*Ubi tres, ibi Ecclesia*). This church is superior to any nation-state because the state asks us to find ourselves only in a patchwork Leviathan, in one massive class or economic system. But for the poet and the leech gatherer there is only the gift of their mutual presence; everything else is to be determined later. Countercultures and counter-churches work by drawing people closer.

But perhaps I don't do Weiwei justice. Perhaps *Human Flow* is about his feelings of distance from the very people who are most like him, who are suffering what he suffered in China. Perhaps the film is a confession of his failure to find a way to meaningful solidarity with the wretched of the earth.

Perhaps the film is about the impotence of his pity.

. . . .

* Or birds. This from Keats: "If a Sparrow comes before my Window, I take part in its existence and pick about the Gravel."

PART
II

pity party

WHAT IS HIDDEN
IN THE SUN'S EYE

There is an old Arabic saying: "If you wish to hide something, hide it in the sun's eye," which is a way of saying that Ai Weiwei's *Human Flow* hides as much as it reveals. Calling Syria, or Gaza, or Sudan failed states obscures the fact that all states are failed states insofar as they fail the basic needs and aspirations of their people. The truth is that Ai Weiwei's status as art celebrity is dependent on his not blurring the line between the successful nations of the West and failed nations elsewhere. If he did blur that line, if he laid everything out in the light of the sun and not in its eye, he would have a much harder time getting funding for his art projects. He can erect a golden fence around the Park Hotel in Manhattan in order to criticize Trump's version of China's Great Wall, but that merely makes him an inside player in the civil war that American oligarchs are fighting among themselves. That's just CNN versus Fox. That's just Soros vs. Koch. Clinton vs. Trump. Or the FBI vs. the Justice Department!

While Weiwei is grateful for the West's artistic and journalistic freedoms and uses them abundantly, what passes without notice is the fact that his freedom of expression is dependent on *not* saying certain things. Not saying, for example, that the plight of refugees is the consequence of the First World's more fundamental freedom—the freedom to fleece the vulnerable, distant populations most severely, obviously, but domestic populations as well. Weiwei may chasten the First World for its lack of compassion, but he does not challenge the dominant narrative that the predicament of the refugees is the consequence of the customs, whether tribal or sectarian, the ancient feuds, the violence, and the corruption of their countries of origin. Meanwhile, "wreckage capitalism"—big oil, mining, big pharma, and industrialized agriculture—goes on with the business of exploitation, paying warlords or duly elected gangsters for access to national resources, including the people themselves. That's what made Rex Tillerson such a natural fit as secretary of state: Exxon was already in the business of administering foreign policy.

Think what a different kind of movie *Human Flow* would have been if Weiwei had sought to show that the line between developed and undeveloped, prosperous and poor, First and Third, was not a line at all, was a distinction without a difference. We, too, are a failed state. We, too, are out of place.

Go somewhere else.

A specter haunts us: whether priced-out, crazy, drunk, opiated, or terminally foolish, we call them the "homeless," and they are many. Of course, the homeless are not a new phenomenon. Charles Dickens knew them well:

> The night was bitter cold . . . Bleak, dark, and piercing cold, it was a night for the well-housed and fed to draw round the bright fire and thank God they were at home; and for the homeless, starving wretch to lay him down and die. Many hunger-worn outcasts close their eyes in our bare streets, at such times, who, let their crimes have been what they may, can hardly open them in a more bitter world. (*Oliver Twist*, 1837)

Still, there is something astonishing about the fact that in 2017 there were fifty-five thousand "street dwellers" in Los Angeles, an increase of 25 percent over the previous year. In a distressing report first published in *The Guardian*, journalist Ed Pilkington accompanied Philip Alston, UN special "rapporteur," on a tour of poverty in the United States:

> We come to an intersection, which is when General Dogon [a local activist] stops and presents his guest with the choice. He points straight ahead to the end of the street, where the glistening skyscrapers of downtown LA rise up in a promise of divine riches.
>
> Heaven.
>
> Then he turns to the right, revealing the "black power" tattoo on his neck, and leads our gaze back into Skid Row bang in the center of LA's downtown. That way lies 50 blocks of concentrated human humiliation. A nightmare in plain view, in the city of dreams.[7]

Like the Middle Eastern immigrants arriving in Europe, the homeless in L.A. are met mostly by "indifference." One resident, Tiny Gray-Garcia, has a telling expression for this indifference: "the violence of looking away." An investigation conducted by the New York City Rescue Mission showed how deeply set this "looking away" is:

> Many city dwellers do their best not to see the homeless people who share their streets and pavements . . . In 2014, the New York City Rescue Mission, a shelter, conducted a social experiment, Make Them Visible, in which they filmed participants walking past relatives disguised as homeless people. None of the participants noticed their relations sitting on the street.[8]

When the number of homeless becomes too great to look away from (fifty blocks, after all), the solution for San Francisco, Los Angeles, Las Vegas, and New York is to hand out free bus tickets to . . . wherever, anywhere but where they are now. Let the homeless themselves choose the destination for their banishment. Let the mayor of Indianapolis figure out what to do with them. Put them in a bus and push them from shore. A "relocation program" like San Francisco's Homeward Bound (as it is cruelly monikered) is the flip side of ICE's concentration camp for immigrant children in Tornillo, Texas. Opposites, but of the same debased currency.

Similarly ghost like are the "left behind," like the sinners in one of Tim LaHaye's rapture novels—the working class in the post-industrial United States. Louisiana is a failed state and so are Youngstown and Dayton, Ohio, and Kimberly, Wisconsin (where ninety thousand factory jobs, mostly in paper mills, have been lost since 2000). Unlike the refugees in Greece or the homeless being moved about the country on Greyhound buses, the left behind aren't going anywhere and they sure aren't "flowing." While San Francisco and Seattle can't build apartments fast enough to house all the new arrivals, the rest of the country is in reverse: 2017 marked the fifth straight year that the share of the population moving to a new place dropped, to 11 percent from as high as 20 percent in 1985, according to the Census Bureau. An aging population of Boomer retirees is part of the reason for this shift, but the young are part of the problem as well. Stricter requirements for mortgages, student debt, and high prices in cities will set up a confrontation between junior and grandma for the use of the basement couch.[9]

Stuck where they are, the left behind are offered only "right to work" conditions where union-free factories pay low wages with high risks. For example, Alabama has sold itself to foreign automakers as the New Detroit, although the work is more like something out of Charlie Chaplin's *Modern Times*. OSHA has documented cases of burning flesh and crushed limbs at auto-parts plants like Ajin in Cusseta, Alabama. In 2015, the chance of losing a finger or limb in an Alabama parts factory was double the amputation risk nationally for the industry. To add insult to literal injury, much of this mayhem comes as a consequence of having to work alongside malfunctioning robots, which say to fellow employees, "If you object to being maimed, we'll simply take your job."

As for those who are not blessed with the brutal benevolence of a Hyundai or Kia plant full of dangerous robots, their lot will be poverty, drug addiction, obesity-related epidemics, early death, and incarceration.* They will be blessed with nothing, nothing to do, nothing to hope for. They are the "not needed" and they are the large part of the epidemic of suicides that moves in lockstep alongside the opioid and meth crisis. It's social inequality Russian style: if these people were living in Siberia, they'd be drinking facial toner. That's despair darker than I know how to do justice to.

The left behind are characters in a damned-if-they-do-damned-if-they-don't tragedy in which all the tragic flaws are systemic, not personal. They are caught between two imponderable forces, like

. . . .

*   According to the Bureau of Justice Statistics, the ten states with the highest incarceration rates are all southern states, led by Louisiana with a rate nearly double the national average (816 per 100,000 in Louisiana versus 417 per 100,000 nationally). Of course, the national figure would be even lower if it excluded prison populations in the South. So, 816 v. 300? Even 300 is a national disgrace.

Odysseus caught between Scylla and Charybdis (the Greek version of "a rock and a hard place"). On one side we have the "progressive" forces of the high-tech economy eliminating ever more of the jobs that used to support middle-class families. Because of Uber and Lyft, the value of a New York taxi medallion has dropped by half and more. Self-driving trucks are on the horizon. A little further off, low maintenance electric cars will eliminate the need for most auto mechanics.*

Now, these putative progressive forces that are running the economy might be willing to do something for the people that they harm. Technocratic elites on the Obama/Clinton axis are open to various kinds of fiscal redistribution, including "Medicare for all" and "guaranteed minimum income" programs. But the willingness to help those they've hurt is not serious. It is a mere "nice thought" because on the other side we have the entrenched forces of accumulated wealth and free market ideology unwilling to do anything for anybody anywhere—and they are running the government. Mitch McConnell wants to gut Medicaid while representing Kentucky, one of the most Medicaid-dependent states in the Union. In

. . . .

* This dynamic is not limited to the left behind; even code writers are at risk. As Toby Walsh, a professor of artificial intelligence at the University of New South Wales, commented to *The Guardian*, "We will eventually give up writing algorithms altogether because the machines will be able to do it far better than we ever could. Software engineering is in that sense perhaps a dying profession" (Andrew Smith, "Franken-algorithms: the deadly consequences of unpredictable code," *The Guardian*, August 30, 2018). Worse yet for yours truly, Elon Musk's OpenAI has announced that its latest AI text-writer, GPT2, can write novels and essays in the voice of any writer given only a single sentence. For example, a sentence like, "This is a book about counterculture, and that's a problem."

Kentucky, you have to work to get Medicaid. In Kentucky, you have to take a course and pass a test to get Medicaid.

As blue states lead a NASDAQ frenzy of state-of-the-art creative destruction, handing ever more categories of work to robots, red states determine national politics and instruct the unemployed and unemployable that they ought to be self-reliant, that their suffering is their own fault. One side takes away work while the other refuses to offer the jobless any aid beyond a part-time minimum wage gig at Burger King.

While the technologic wonders of the modern world are displayed all around the left behind, it feels to them as if they are suffering internal exile in some Third World country of the soul. This is not a new experience for the dispossessed of the earth. Nathanael West described their condition lucidly in *The Day of the Locust* (1939):

> Scattered among these [wealthy] masqueraders were people of a different type. Their clothing was somber and badly cut, bought from mail-order houses. While the others moved rapidly, darting into stores and cocktail bars, they loitered on the corners or stood with their backs to the shop windows and stared at everyone who passed. When their stare was returned, their eyes filled with hatred.

Our outsiders, like West's, have few means of responding to their dispossession. As a consequence, they will continue to be an easy mark for political conmen, and they will continue to send their own private Attilas to the White House and Congress, elected because they promised to "blow up" something—the establishment, the Republican Party, something, anything. They will continue to vote for candidates who in any other context would be considered sociopaths. Voting becomes an expression of the desire for revenge against a world that has humiliated them intellectually, economically, sexually, racially, and, through the opulent creations that the left behind gazes upon from an alien distance, aesthetically. Unhappily, this socio-pathology will be first and foremost visited upon their own disconsolate heads.

Many on the liberal side of the political spectrum continue to think that these disconsolate heads are disconsolate because they are also stupid. They think that all that is required to end the present "idiocracy" is to exert their own intelligence. Nathanael West was aware of the same things we see in Trump supporters, the same "drained-out, feeble bodies" and "wild, disordered minds," but, unlike present-day liberals, West was not smug and dismissive. Instead, he "[depicted] their fury with respect, appreciating its awful, anarchic power and aware that they had it in them to destroy civilization."

Add to the left behind the "precariat," those who have a perch in the prosperous West, for the moment, even if that perch is in "wheel estate": RVs, travel trailers, vans, and pickup campers. This nomad population serves as temporary labor in agriculture, but also seasonally for Amazon in a program it calls CamperForce. These vulnerable workers are the result of domestic outsourcing; they are not employees but contract workers for McJobs.

Think of the battered RVs of these nomads as our own First World version of the North Korean "ghost ships" that wash up on the Japanese coastline with their gruesome cargoes of dead refugees and fishermen. Invisible to demographers, our domestic refugees survive only as long as Social Security, Medicare, and the rear axle on their '95 Lazy Daze RV survive. If those things go, Amazon has no intention of making up the difference. CamperForce nomads might then look for a refugee's raft (if they could think of some place to float to).

And what if Weiwei had included the movement of the so-called "cognitariat" (or "knowledge workers") from rural and Rust Belt states to urban technology centers, creating what libertarian social scientist Charles Murray has called, approvingly, the "secession of the successful" in "a new kind of segregation."[10] This movement is leaving archetypal small-town America behind and throwing those who have left into a future that would be prosperous if it weren't for the fact that they still have enormous rents to pay and giant student loans to repay. As Michael Hobbes wrote for *HuffPost's Highline*:

> This leaves young people, especially those without a college degree, with an impossible choice. They can move to a city where there are good jobs but insane rents. Or they can move somewhere with low rents but few jobs that pay above the minimum wage.[11]

On December 30, 2017, Jennifer Phipps became the face of this predicament (for that day's news cycle) with an op-ed in *The Seattle Times* titled "In Seattle, a 2-bedroom apartment for a single mom is but a dream." She has a "good job" working as a program coordinator at the University of Washington, but she and her nine-year-old son must live in a studio apartment for which she pays more than 65 percent of her net monthly pay.

> Last month the UW Self-Sufficiency Standard for the state of Washington released a report that revealed the scope of my

problem. In Seattle, the cost of meeting basic needs increased
thirty thousand dollars in a decade. For a family to make it in
Seattle, parents must make seventy-five thousand dollars annually just to exist. Not to live well. To exist . . . I can subsist for
just one more lease.*

On the same day that Phipp's op-ed appeared in *The Seattle Times*,
Bloomberg News published an article by Christopher Flavelle suggesting that "Florida's real-estate reckoning could be closer than
you think." In Coral Gables and Biscayne Bay, the elite seaside ref-
uges for our economic winners, the psychology of homeowners is
turning grim: There's not enough land, high enough above the water, for residents to pull back from rising seas. By the end of the
century, database company Zillow Group estimates, almost five
hundred thousand Miami homes could be literally underwater.[12]

Apparently, we must now add the most unexpected refugees,
joining nomad populations in Africa, the Middle East, and on the
streets of L.A.: millionaires. Millionaires in Miami and millionaires
sleeping on cots in county fairgrounds in Los Angeles, Santa Rosa,
and Redding, sobbing beneath dust masks after wildfires have destroyed their dream homes and cars. According to Orrin Pilkey,
author of *Sea Level Rise: the Slow Tsunami on America's Shores*,[13] the
millionaire migrants of the future "will not be the bedraggled
families carrying their few possessions on their backs . . . Instead,
they will be well-off Americans driving to a new life in their cars,
with moving trucks behind, carrying a lifetime of memories and
possessions."[14]

· ·

* Also, see M. H. Miller's student debt confessional, "Been Down So Long It
Looks Like Debt to Me," *The Baffler*, No. 40, July 2018.

These refugees are our "winners," people who once imagined that, as Bob Dylan sang, their "gladness had come to pass." But that gladness is presently moving from a prestigious beach address in Miami Beach to low-income Little Haiti, which has discovered the advantages of being a few more feet above sea level. Real estate "price signals" say sell the surfside mansion and buy the uptown teardown, a swap now known as "climate gentrification." Given estimates for rising sea levels in the next century, a more literal example of "rearranging deck chairs on the Titanic" is difficult to imagine.

These diverse domestic populations cannot be included in the official version of the refugee crisis, something that happens in faraway Greece, because it would obscure the line between us. We are prosperous, orderly, a nation of laws and rights, even while most people who actually live here, up and down the "status hierarchy"—the homeless, the left behind, the precariat, the cognitariat, and now even millionaires—feel something very different. Like the Syrian refugees marooned in Turkey (or, worse, in the Australian concentration camps on Manus Island), we have little control over our futures. Abandoned in what John de Graaf aptly calls the "you're on your ownership society," we are responsible for our own education, housing, and health, even while those things are indecently expensive, especially in those places where we must live in order to have one of the "good jobs," which are themselves no more secure than the next turn of the Silicon screw. (Žižek: "The weird coexistence of intense employment with the threat of unemployment.") Precarity has become a generalized existential condition for all of us. It defines both winners and losers, millionaires and the homeless. The next Wall Street bubble, and the next winter "bomb cyclone" that will have Florida's iguanas dropping lifeless from the trees, are the Revenge of the Real.

Worse yet is the fact that our domestic refugee populations have much in common and yet they are incurably separate. Homelessness is one system, precarity another. The cognitariat has no allegiance to flooded or burned-out millionaires. Unlike the 19th and 20th centuries, when one could plausibly appeal to a unitary "working class," what we have now are essentially separate systems of wretchedness in a social context that is radically anti-communal. That's not a happy fact, but it is a fact.

Where does all of this leave us? The New Deal's dream of a liberal welfare state working within a mixed economy—a regulated capitalism—is eroding, one Republican budget at a time. The United States has returned to its oligarchic origins with a vengeance. Sure, gays can get married and pot is more or less legal, but the oligarchs don't care about that stuff. Light up a joint and fuck yourself silly, they say. Meanwhile, well over 50 percent of the population lives on an annual income of thirty thousand dollars or less, and, meanwhile, wealth concentrates at the top, ever denser, as if the sad mass of the rest of the country were being used to make a diamond.

PART
III

Cowards

2 cant do it so 7'll while

COUNTERCULTURE IS IMPERTINENT

In response to this ongoing crisis of displacement, both international and domestic, the question that we are all asking now is, as Tolstoy put it, "What is to be done?" Socialist revolution? Get the Republican ladies in the suburbs to vote blue?

In a trenchant overview of the world post-Brexit and post-Trump—"From Progressive Neo-liberalism to Trump—and Beyond"—Nancy Fraser concludes that we are in the midst of a "crisis of hegemony." The dominant "hegemonic bloc" for the last forty years, since Reagan, has been neoliberal. For Fraser, this means "financialization": removal of trade barriers, deregulation of banking, predatory debt, deindustrialization, weak unions, and the spread of low wage and precarious work. But what the last few years have shown is that the neo-liberal script no longer compels belief and, as a consequence, no longer provides legitimacy. As Fraser writes, "It is as if masses of people throughout the world had stopped believing in the reigning common sense that underpinned political domination for the last several decades." It's in this psychological context that we must understand Trump, Brexit, the weakening of the EU, and the rise of authoritarian regimes in Poland, Hungary, Turkey, and elsewhere.

Fraser's essay goes into considerable detail about the options remaining to us. The old neo-liberal order could yet be re-established through the "progressive neo-liberalism" of the Clintons and

Obama in a familiar do-si-do relationship with the "reactionary neo-liberalism" of the mainstream Republican Party, but Fraser's perception is that this queer neo-liberal alliance is precisely what has been so dramatically rejected. The alternative to neo-liberalism is populism: Bernie Sanders's progressive populism or Trump's hyper-reactionary populism. Fraser's hope is that progressive populism can begin to form a "counterhegemonic bloc" with working class elements of the Trump bloc that "could end up being transitional—a way station en route to some new, post-capitalist form of society."[15]

This is about as good as a purely political analysis of the situation is going to get, but it is also a political analysis that does not know how to think *beyond* politics . . . and there *is* something beyond politics. It is what we do every day when we're not thinking about how fucked up politics are. We call it food, we call it home, we call it recreation, and we call it art, but mostly we call it culture.

What I want to emphasize here, something that politics-as-usual ignores, is culture-as-politics. I have already suggested this in my account of Varda and JR's *Faces Places*, a film that is politically important for at least three reasons. First, the film itself is formally *disobedient*. It misbehaves. It crosses the boundaries between the personal and the public, the artistic and the social. Second, it creates an alternative world that is, especially in comparison to the world we have, strikingly *beautiful*, which is to say desirable. Third, it sharpens our appetite for *winning*, for actually having the world that the film suggests. In that important sense it is revolutionary, or perhaps the better word, because of the violent connotations of "revolution," is *insurrectionary*. As Max Stirner wrote in *The Ego and Its Own* (1844):

Revolution and insurrection must not be looked upon as syn-
onymous . . . [Insurrection] is not an armed uprising, but a
rising of individuals, a getting up, without regard to the arrangements that spring from it. The Revolution aimed at new
arrangements; insurrection leads us to no longer let ourselves
be arranged, but to arrange ourselves, and sets no glittering
hopes on "institutions."

Counterculture is such a "getting up," an insurrection in the name
of life.

Contrary to what the mass media would have us believe, culture is
not merely the customs, language, religion, and cuisine of a place.
Nor is culture merely the movies, the music, the Internet of Things,
and the rest of capitalist life's fabulously stippled frou-frous. These
are very static ways of thinking about culture. And certainly culture
is not the mechanically produced "superstructure," the pale reflection of an economic "base," of Marxist materialism.

Properly understood, culture is concerned with the process of
becoming. Culture is about movement more fundamental than this
year's political movements. As Sigmund Freud wrote, culture is the
act of "replacing what is unconscious with what is conscious." A
cult is unconscious. It simply does what it has always done. It fol-
lows instructions. Culture, on the other hand, is the bringing to
awareness of the damage—the repression, irrationality, violence,
ugliness, injustice, and tragedy—imposed by the cult. In this sense,
culture is enlightenment.

And in this sense the United States is a cult.

A cult is not capable of Freud's enlightenment. It has only its
crude and cruel version of eternity: "This is how we do this, we

have always done it this way, we will always do it this way, this is not negotiable, it is not worth thinking about let alone talking about, it just is, and, by the way, shut up or else." If you are in Saudi Arabia, do not write blogs seeking to open a frank discussion of Islam or you will go to jail: a very unpleasant jail, and jailers with whips for lashing. And if you're in Thailand, do not insult the king, or even his mongrel pet dog, or you will go to jail: a very unpleasant jail, and "etcetera, etcetera, and so forth," as a fictional King of Siam once put it. The cult enforces what is to be done through constant reference to what has already been done, and, as we know, it is deadly serious about its enforcement responsibilities. Disgracefully, these foreign outrages are not at all foreign on our shores, especially if you are an immigrant confronted by the cult of "America First."

Cults also take more sophisticated forms. In the United States at present, most of what passes for culture is, by Freud's understanding, not culture at all. This is especially true for our art—it's not art at all. It's not that it is "bad" art, it's that it is merely an expression of a cult, New York's cult of capitalist realism, say, when it comes to novel writing. Our novels, our television dramas, our movies, and our music are *mostly* cult-like determinations not to think, not to be self-reflective, and certainly not to change. Cult art wants only to continue to be what it has been. It doesn't want you to tell it how conformist and dull it is; it only wants you to celebrate its "blockbusters." And celebrate it does, as Hollywood's 2016 auto-fellation over *La La Land* and *Kong: Skull Island* demonstrated yet again.

It's not that a critical language for describing a conscious, or enlightened, culture of art is completely lacking. It appears at times, but usually only if the art happens where it is unlikely to be seen. Culture can do whatever it wants so long as it acts out its enlightened intentions in a closet. Consider this from a review by *New York Times* critic Anthony Tommasini of composer Andrew Norman's "Split," performed in December of 2015, in New York:

> The radical element . . . is the way Mr. Norman handles time and structure. His feel for storytelling is permeated by "nonlinear, narrative-scrambling techniques from cinema, television and video games," as he explains on his website. So his music can seem like nonstop quick cuts from one idea to another . . . Sometimes the piano broke into spiraling flourishes, like Ravel gone vehement, or arpeggio madness.[16]

Of course, the experience of the radical potential of this music—which is to say the potential of the music to change the terms of American life—is limited to the moneyed connoisseurs who finance both it and the extravagant gathering places—David Geffen Hall, David Koch Theater—where the music is performed. This state of affairs became a national news story when the Broadway producers of *Hamilton* raised the price of a ticket to $849 in an effort to frustrate "ticket bot" scalpers who were selling seats for an average of one thousand dollars. The managers of this theatrical franchise reasoned that by reducing the profit margin for the bots they would eliminate the incentive to "scalp" while capturing more of the market value for the real owners of the theatrical property. Of course, while the gymnastics of price setting may have helped further reward *Hamilton*'s investors, it did nothing to make the show affordable for those without a few thousand bucks to spend on an evening's entertainment. In the end, the ticket bots understand something about the nature of American culture that the producers do not: art is not for everyone, just as the stock market is not for everyone.

The sophisticates who can afford culture operate not only in bad faith, but in the worst possible faith because they turn the experience of what ought to be liberating into a mere demonstration of their superiority—their superiority for being able to afford the ticket, first, but also their superiority for being able to "appreciate" what is difficult. It is in such cases that the complaint of "elitism" coming from red-state populists makes perfect sense. These populists should say, "You use art to confirm your right to wealth and power." The virtue of understanding what is difficult is the second half of the brutal equation that goes, "I deserve to be rich because I've *earned* it," as John Houseman used to scold, "and *I'm smarter than you*." The concert that Tommasini described was a ritual display of culture in the service of a cult.

Such displays legitimize the continued domination of those whom the oligarchs think of as, essentially, their servants—the salary men, the data drudges, and workers with "bullshit jobs"*—exactly those for whom the liberating effect of the music *should* have been intended and, I hope, would have been intended if Mr. Norman had any say in the matter. On the other hand, if the art in question were more popular, if it were something that tried to thrive outside of the oligarchy's art temples, it would know better than to exhibit "narrative scrambling" and "arpeggio madness."

There are filters for that sort of thing. As aspiring novelists discover early on, instruction in university writing workshops is *mostly* oriented toward domestic or social realism (we called the University of Iowa Writers Workshop the "Field and Stream School of Writing"

. . . .

* David Graeber: "It's as if someone were out there making up pointless jobs just for the sake of keeping us all working."

back in my student days). A university workshop apprenticeship is followed closely by agents, editors, and, at the end of the line, the publisher and his executive staff (Rupert Murdoch, after all, owns HarperCollins), all of whom have internalized a certain commercial aesthetic: "Nothing too literary or difficult! Nothing too weird! Nothing too radical!"

In other words, nothing that might tend to suggest that there are other ways of ordering reality, exactly what art is supposed to do, and did in fact do beginning with the Romantic revolutionaries and continuing through the druggy bliss of a century and a half of art's various –isms, from symbolism, expressionism, and surrealism to the Beats and psychedelia. These were not elite exercises in difficult art; they were first and foremost *social* movements whose purpose was to reinvent religion (Blake), confound the bourgeois (Baudelaire and Flaubert), or "freak out" (the Dada-inspired Mothers of Invention). As Frank Zappa wrote in the liner notes to the album *Freak Out*:

> What is *"Freaking Out"*? . . . On a collective level, when any number of *"Freaks"* gather and express themselves creatively through music or dance, for example, it is generally referred to as a *Freak Out*. The participants, already emancipated from our national *social slavery*, dressed in their most inspired apparel, realize as a group whatever potential they possess for *free expression*.

In the present, unfortunately, most of the art that does freak out a bit, that does foreground arpeggio madness, is no threat to social slavery because it is mostly elite sophisticates—who have no intention of changing anything—who are exposed to its challenges.

But, of course, they misrecognize these challenges and call them pleasure, or profit, or "this season's triumph"—for sophisticates only. What the rest of us get, outside the charmed circle of Alice Tully Hall, is carefully managed to make sure it affirms again and again capitalism's unrelenting *mysterium*, home to the cult of the Market God and his invisible hand, which keeps itself busy counting out the stars in Amazon reader reviews, ad infinitum.

Without question, these observations will be met with resistance by many within our nascent Resistance to all things Trump-like. They will offer their own observation that, no, I'm quite wrong, culture is still a leading aspect of the fight against the oligarchs, the dupes, and the neo-fascist flunkies. Why, the cast of *Hamilton* confronted the vice president of the United States, Mike Pence, when he attended a performance and sat in his thousand-dollar seat. And they will suggest that *Hamilton* and the many recent books, movies, memoirs, and novels addressed to social issues are a sign that American culture is vital and is throwing itself powerfully against the reign of right-wing billionaires.

But much of this resistance is the same old mass media sludge. Michael Wolff's takedown of Donald Trump, *Fire and Fury*, was an important book in part *because* it was a gossipy tell-all. It was not an important book because it had something revealing to say about our neoliberal oligarchs. *Fire and Fury* is the kind of opposition that makes billions of dollars for corporations. As William Rivers Pitt wrote in one of his many revealing columns for *Truthout*:

> Let's remember, though, that [*Fire and Fury*] is also a confection for the media, grist for the mill, cash money. Mainstream

media outlets, clearly, are not at all tired of all this winning. We're trapped in a bad plot we didn't write, binge-watching history as the ratings soar.[17]

To this might well be added the intellectual resistance provided by corporate media giants MSNBC (owned by Comcast) and CNN (AT&T), and through newsroom celebrities like Rachel Maddow, Chris Hayes, and Don Lemon. These celebrities provide Trump soap opera, the present stimulating version of the Society of the Spectacle, the revolution that wasn't supposed to be televised this time. Rachel Maddow will always be smart, analytical, and entertaining, on or off TV, but she'll be on TV only as long as she's profitable. Many of her viewers may imagine that by watching her show they are participating in the "Resistance," but in the end they're "boxed in," in Mark Crispin Miller's phrase: they're merely watching TV.

Or going to the movies.

As if to provide an exclamation point for these thoughts, here comes Ryan Coogler's *Black Panther* (2018). The popular and critical enthusiasm for this film's liberating effects was, for the purposes of independent thought, almost suffocating, and that in spite of the fact that so much of the film was an orgy of political guilty pleasures provided by the Hollywood aesthetic which says "violence is good as long as it's virtuosic"; by the glorification of technology, especially military technology (the James Bond allusions are unsubtle); and by the uncritical endorsement of problem-solving billionaire philanthropists (King T'Challa buys up and rehabs buildings in Oakland in the film's final scene).

The elevation of billionaires as liberators is the guiltiest of the film's guilty pleasures. The movie offers the idea that benevolent autocrat warrior heroes provide better answers to world problems than the *demos*, than the people affected, especially the African American community. On dangerous fantasies about autocrats, Timothy Egan has this to say in a *New York Times* op-ed:

> It's fine to swoon over the Marvel Comics monarch of Wakanda in *Black Panther*, but a real-life facsimile is dreadful. That would be King Mswati III of Swaziland, the last absolute monarch of sub-Saharan Africa. He has 15 wives and 13 palaces — or maybe it's the other way around — and is worth in excess of $50 million. This while his tiny landlocked kingdom has one of the lowest life expectancies in the world, and the average person gets by on less than $1.50 a day.[18]

This is not the film's only distortion. In the world of *Black Panther* the CIA is represented by a scrawny, feckless white guy . . . but he's on our side! (At least it wasn't the FBI, the murderers of Black Panther Fred Hampton . . . but might's'well've been?) And in the world of *Black Panther,* the revolutionary kid from the hood who would have been a real Black Panther back in the day, that kid is the villain!

And yet in the heady months after the release of the film very few of these concerns seemed to register among viewers and critics who praised the movie's inclusiveness. And indeed, for once black kids could see themselves not as victims but as superheroes. Yes, the filmmakers took a white guy's thin fantasy of a black superhero and pumped it up with what Rahsaan Roland Kirk called "Blacknuss." I get that, and I agree it's an improvement over the usual Stan Lee white leading-man machismo. But should we just do a long glissando over the rest of this stuff? As Christopher Lebron put it in his unerring review, "*Black Panther* is not the movie we deserve."[19]

The lesson from all this is clear: you can have your revolt as long as in all of the important ways it reflects the values of the dominant culture, and the most important of those values, as everyone connected to the *Black Panther* project could tell you, is *make a lot of money*, and, boy, didn't they just.*

Black Panther lands way inside the white culture comfort zone, and bows to the values of that culture, in a way that *Moonlight, Get Out*, or anything by Spike Lee, especially *Bamboozled* and the recent *BlacKkKlansman*, do not. Speaking of Spike Lee, where in the film is there a smart little guy who speaks truth to power, so that the future is not all up to Afro-futurist gladiators? Don't say Shuri (Letitia Wright), the girl genius behind all the superfly James Bond gizmos. The sad joke there is that in the real world the people who have the latest military hardware, the people who look like they're wearing T'Challa's Black Panther body armor, are the TAC squads confronting Black Lives Matter demonstrations.

But perhaps this is only how a white-guy ideology critic reads the movie, and not at all how a black audience reads it. Perhaps it's just me white-mansplaining. As Osha Neumann smartly observed in his review in *CounterPunch*:

. . . .

*   On that note: really distressing to see the great Forest Whitaker doing his Marlon Brando/Jor-El turn as a superhero patriarch. But if he was going to betray his own super-sized talent for cash, he could at least have been paid on Brando's pay scale: Brando made $4 million for his cameo in *Superman*, while Whitaker took in $600,000, and Brando's four large was in 1970 dollars.

As in Hollywood gangster movies, the message has to be that crime against white supremacy does not pay. But that may not matter. Perhaps all the CGI supersized razzle-dazzle whiz bang of the Marvel superhero franchise is what is needed to animate the snarling [Black Panther] to leap into the 21st century. And perhaps at the next urban uprising, Black men and women who have dim memories of that old panther, will stand against phalanxes of police, emboldened by images of Wakanda.[20]

But even that evaluation is optimistic. It's more likely that most black folk, like most white folk, don't mind Hollywood, don't mind beautiful bodies, don't mind feats of martial grandeur (if only as fantasy), don't mind razzle-dazzle technology, don't mind having money and power, don't mind thinking that their nation is superior to and more sophisticated than other nations—it's just that they'd prefer to be the subject, rather than object, of all that force. The idea of inclusiveness is a double-edged sword: don't want to exclude people, but not sure of the good of including them in something so corrupt.

In short, the work of our so-called Resistance is self-limiting, if not utterly self-cancelling. At the very least, it is *constrained*. The radicalness of *Black Panther* is constrained. The news shows, books, and movies that currently give direction to resistance do not do enough to challenge, in Freud's terms, the American unconscious (its cult), which is capitalist, consumerist, scientistic, journalistic, and, worse yet, *sensationalistic*—something for the hallway after class. ("Russian prostitutes made peepee in Donald Trump's hair!") The problem here is that part of the "weakness" of this historical moment is precisely its normality, its conformity to what is thought to be possible or permissible. If the filmmakers, novelists, and critics of our Resistance have defected to some degree from mainstream political culture, that culture has, in turn, taken its revenge by pressing home its demands in the very place that the defectors have sought refuge . . . in the work itself. *Black Panther* obeys the rules for the proper making of superhero flicks. In this formal propriety, the work offers the following assurance to its professed enemies: It won't go *too far*. It won't freak out. The world that awaits us at the end of our Resistance as presently constituted is finally a *familiar* world, and will remain a familiar world, so long as our arbiters of taste are Hollywood, Netflix, the Grammys, *SNL*, CNN, MSNBC, the National Book Awards, and *The New York Times* bestseller list. In short, this lauded resistance is no revolution; it is a form of what Nancy Fraser has identified as progressive neoliberalism.

And just what might a more enlightened film look like? There are many to choose from even now. Jordan Peele's 2017 *Get Out* brilliantly subverts the horror genre for the purpose of letting white folk know how they're seen by African Americans: they're scary. And Spike Lee's films are formally as well as socially radical. They are strongly driven by Lee's authorial voice, not only in his first film, *She's Gotta Have It* (1986) (inspired by Kurosawa's *Rashomon*, of all wonderful things), but throughout his impressive and uncompromising oeuvre.

Still, film culture has fallen a long way from the radicalizing effects of the independent directors of the 1950s, '60s, and '70s (among whom was Agnès Varda). Let me recall the work of the late Nicolas Roeg (he died at ninety in 2018). Roeg is most famous for his rock star vehicles of the '70s, *Performance* (starring Mick Jagger) and *The Man Who Fell to Earth* (starring David Bowie), but he also made two lesser-known films—*Walkabout* (1971) and *Glastonbury Fayre* (1972). *Walkabout* is the story of a young woman and her younger brother lost in the outback of Australia following the bizarre suicide of their father. (He was driven to it by the emptiness of his domestic life and his equally empty work as a corporate geologist.) While trying to walk back to the city, the two desperate children meet an Aborigine youth on his "walkabout," a rite of passage in which the adolescent boy must survive on his own in the desert for a period of months while transitioning to manhood.

The narrative details of this film are rich and varied, but I must be brief: in the process of telling this survival story Roeg eviscerates Western culture for its corporate tedium, its racism, its sexism, and its environmental destructiveness. Without apology, he shows the world of the Aborigine as happier, more beautiful, far less destructive, and more *loyal*, a loyalty that the young woman does not share: in the conclusion she betrays her dark-skinned savior by abandoning his dead body and returning to the suburban horror that had driven her father to suicide.

Crucially, *Walkabout* takes its political critique of the West into the formal properties of the film itself. Unlike *Black Panther*, it is not constrained to create a commercially viable product. *Walkabout* is formally radical. It uses narrative discontinuity, surreal jump cuts, and cinematic framing that are every bit as *avant* as anything Michelangelo Antonioni was making at the time. (The film reminds me in some ways of Antonioni's *Zabriskie Point*.)

Walkabout is an elliptical montage (the cinematic version of "arpeggio madness"?). While watching this film you know that you are not watching a Hollywood movie, or a Netflix movie; in fact, you know that you are watching a movie that *could not be made at all* in the present. This is so because the film is not only critical of social ills (something tolerated by neo-liberalism), but also corrosive of Western consciousness—its crass materialism, its rationalism, its realism—and *that* is beyond the pale.

Interestingly, Roeg's next film was a documentary, *Glastonbury Fayre*, but it reads like a sequel to *Walkabout*. If *Walkabout* is a film that mourns an outback paradise lost, and that mourns the young heroine's decision to return to Western life, *Glastonbury Fayre* is about people trying to recreate a primitive paradise in the West, in England. In genre, it is a "rockumentary," a Celtic Woodstock (the Glastonbury Festival continues to this day, although in a more commercial mode). What's interesting is that Roeg clearly sees that the hippy youth at the festival are trying not to make the decision that the young girl made in *Walkabout*. They're not going back to suburbia, not going back to capitalism (or not yet), and not going back to racism and sexism. Many, many allowances must be made for the flopping breasts and penises, mud dives, goofy mysticism, and generally druggy delirium, but Roeg seems forgiving of all that, enraptured as he is by the spirit of the moment and the opportunities it provides for visual gorgeosity of light and color and movement. What's more, he seems to understand that the "kids are alright" (as The Who sang) because they have no choice except to make it up on the fly, improvising, trying things. This was generally true of the '60s counterculture as a whole: it was thrown into a requirement to invent its world very suddenly. And so, for Roeg, the "Idea" that the Fayre represents is more important than the specifics of this one performance.

It is like the philosophy of G.W.F. Hegel: there is the Idea, what we're trying to make real (what he grandly if vaguely called the Absolute), and then there is the specific "moment," an attempt to achieve the Idea, something that is always partial, never complete. Similarly for Roeg, *Fayre* provides what *Walkabout* mourned the lack of: it creates a form of consciousness that is radically other than the Western capitalist model, but it does so in ways that are, in Hegel's telling phrase, "inadequate to its own purposes." In simpler terms, whatever Idea it is that the Fayre represents, its rendering of that Idea is not good enough. The remedy for this failure is not to give up but to try again, hopefully getting closer to the Idea with each effort. The "logic" of those moments, those failures, is the essence of the story that Hegel's *Phenomenology of Spirit* (1807) has to tell. Hegel's Absolute is like the horizon, a direction we can go in, but not a place where we arrive. The same should be understood for counterculture: it is not a utopian destination but a process of becoming.

Freud's idea of culture as coming-to-consciousness wants something more than a return to what is customary. It wants something more than to be admired by wealth or vindicated by inclusion in a museum, canon, or repertoire, the "therapeutic institutions" (Dave Hickey) where art is immobilized, caught in amber, and hung on the wall. What Freud's culture asks for is to be understood for what it is—*impertinent*: unrestrained by the dominant notions of what is appropriate; insolent, as needed; and irrelevant to what the bosses think is important. (Wasn't his foregrounding of sex, especially childhood sexuality, impertinent to Victorian sensibilities in this sense? "Dr. Freud, that sort of talk is inappropriate.") Art is impertinent because it meddles in what is beyond its proper sphere. It is not content to remain within the narrow scope of art-as-entertainment even if it is allowed to carry the outraged bone of social commentary in its mouth. The culture of impertinence intends to seduce its audiences to join in its impertinence, and so into the Paris night we go after the first performance of *The Rite of Spring* in 1902, or outside the Whiskey a Go Go with Zappa and his Mothers in 1967, or into the mosh pit for the Pixies' "Debaser" in 1989, or into the "Dadaist temporary autonomous zone" (just outside Reno, if you're wondering) for Burning Man in 1990.

The culture of impertinence scorns the awards offered by the oligarchs,* for which scorn it is properly scorned in return by capitalism's Culture Industry. But that is expected. What is more discouraging is the scorn that comes from those who should have something to gain from art's impertinences, those whom Zappa called "social slaves." The servant class—a "passively rotting mass," as Marx called it—says, "It's admirable and virtuous to survive by the rules that our masters set. It's not easy to follow instructions. Don't you elitists—you liberals, you Jews, you professors, you artists—tell us that you're going to change all the rules now, or redeem us, or enlighten us, or whatever it is you have in mind. We will *hate* you for the effort." Here, the slave supports the interests of the master, creating a cult that means not only the slave's defeat but human defeat.

The Romantic philosopher Friedrich Schlegel thought that this cult, this odd alliance of master and slave, was governed by the

. . . .

* The most impertinent Swedish pop group The Knife sent two people in gorilla costumes to represent them at the 2003 Grammy Awards. There were no such scenes at the Oscars for *Black Panther*, in spite of the fact that M'Baku was king of the nation of Man-Apes.

Axiom of the Average. In *Critical Fragments* (1797), Schlegel wrote:

> The Axiom of the Average: as we and our surroundings are, so must it have been always and everywhere, because that, after all, is so very natural.

For the cult, this Axiom is a *morality*, a morality whose primary virtue is its indiscussability. But this is a morality that, as Nietzsche remarked, "makes stupid." We think that we are better people if we conform to the expectations of religion, capitalism, two party politics, and commercial art. But we do not make ourselves better, we make ourselves stupid.

Of course, it is impertinent to say so.

The one thing that I would add to Freud's observation about culture-as-consciousness is that, understood in this way (as the opposite of cult-as-unconsciousness), culture really always means *counter*-culture: authentic culture is always *in opposition* to everything that is governed by the Axiom of the Average . . . and that includes woke black superheroes.

Of course, it is important not to reduce a moral problem to an aesthetic one, but what I am arguing has nothing to do with taste in art, whether good, bad, or indifferent. What I am proposing is a more general exit from a certain history—or, as Timothy Leary famously suggested at the beginning of the first great iteration of counterculture American style—*dropping out* of that history. Listen to Robert Musil in his novel *The Man Without Qualities* (1933):

> This business of serving as "the stuff of history" infuriated Ulrich [the novel's protagonist]. The luminous, swaying box [a train] in which he was riding seemed to be a machine in which

several hundred kilos of people were being rattled around, by way of being processed into "the future." A hundred years earlier they had sat in a mail coach with the same look on their faces, and a hundred years hence, whatever was going on, they would be sitting as new people in exactly the same way in their updated transport machines—he was revolted by this lethargic acceptance of changes and conditions, this helpless contemporaneity, this mindlessly submissive, truly demeaning stringing along with the centuries, just as if he were suddenly rebelling against the hat, curious enough in shape, that was sitting on his head.

Ulrich is the "man without qualities," but everyone in the novel, in the Austria of 1913, lacked qualities. What was inside their heads, what was worn on their heads, the world they moved about in, it was all merely the filler of the historical moment. Where Ulrich is unique is in *knowing* he lacks qualities. His tragedy is that he never figures out how to acquire them. But the same was not true of Musil himself because, unlike the "good Germans" of his moment—the monarchists, the bureaucrats, the capitalists, and the fascists—he found a way to create his unique qualities by writing the novel *The Man Without Qualities*. He stepped out of history and paid a heavy personal price for it: banned by the Nazis, exiled, impoverished, and mostly ignored (except for the extraordinary devotion of Thomas Mann). But he was loyal to something that was worth being loyal to, his *qualities*, that is to say, his art. Surely, he should stand for us—in our moment, the coach door of history standing open before us, our seats ready—as a prophet. His lesson? His lesson was what we said to draftees during the Vietnam War upon arriving at the Oakland induction center: Don't step forward.

Refuse conscription. While we're at it, refuse social regimentation through work. Refuse consumerism and the destruction that comes with it. You first

Refuse to get on Musil's train.

Refuse.

The politics of refusal begins with the refusal of our own symbolic universe, what Nietzsche called our "inherited stupidities."* If we are to create new cultures and new subjectivities, we must leave behind the old. This is the most general form of refusal and the most difficult because it means refusing what feels like our innermost being. It means refusing to be a "good German," a "loyal employee," a "dutiful soldier," or a "patriotic American." It is what Marx meant when he said that communism required the "ruthless critique of everything existing." It is what Nietzsche meant by the "transvaluation of all values." As he put it, "What is needed above all is an absolute skepticism toward all inherited concepts." It is what Jesus meant when he said, "If anyone comes to me and does not hate father and mother, wife and children, brothers and sisters—yes, even their own life—such a person cannot be my disciple." Jesus was asking his followers to abandon the symbolic universe into which they happened to be born, in the name of a truer and a morally superior way of life. Buddhism calls it karma, all the habits and delusions

- -

* Nietzsche was neither the first nor the last to use this idea. In *Bouvard et Pécuchet* (1881), Gustave Flaubert called inherited stupidities "*idées reçues*," "received ideas." The symbolist poet Remy de Gourmont called them "shells of thought," things for crabs to crawl into. Or the literary critic Hugh Kenner: "They are the masks of culture . . . literacy consists in strapping one on and speaking one's banalities through its orifice."

that carry from generation to generation, creating what Carl Jung termed our destructive "collective shadow."

If the '60s were revolutionary in any sense at all, it was in stepping out of this destructive "shadow" through the refusal of inherited cultural identity. In this it was no failure, and no disappointment. This refusal was the substance of the so-called generation gap that pitted children against parents. Much to their parents' pain, the children of the counterculture radically debunked the reigning platitudes of nation, religion, gender, race, marriage, work, success, war, nature, and onward and ever upward. Most importantly, the counterculture debunked the idea that art, especially music, was about entertainment. Not at all. As Grace Slick of the Jefferson Airplane sang, thinking of Vietnam but channeling James Joyce, "I'd rather have my country die for me." That sentiment, expressed in a popular song, is entertainment's beyond.

The Airplane's brilliant album *After Bathing at Baxter's* participates in what, during the early days of the Russian Revolution, was called a "war on signs": Bolsheviks destroyed statues and other symbols of czarist rule. Something like that war on signs is presently taking place through the removal of monuments to the Confederacy in city parks across the South, leading to the creation of the organization "Decolonize This Place." The #MeToo movement is a war on signs: the Dustin Hoffman celebrity idol is permanently tarnished. Al Franken, Bill Cosby, Kevin Spacey, and, obviously, Harvey Weinstein are fallen idols, toppled with all the subtlety of a bronze Lenin doing a half twist in the pike position in Prague, 1989.

So, yes, tear down the statues and fire the Hollywood stars. But we need a war against *all* of the signs that make up American consciousness. There may well be some of these signs that we keep in the end, but until this great disaster machine we inhabit can explain to us why we shouldn't, let's enforce what the Greeks called *epoché*: let's "withhold consent." In a word, let's *refuse*.

So, it's not like Bruce Willis said in *Die Hard*. It's not yippee-yi-ki-yay.

It's goo-goo-ga-joob, motherfucker.

you first,

AN IMPERTINENT IMPROVISATION: IN PRAISE OF STUPIDITY

"Against stupidity, the gods themselves fight in vain."
—Friedrich Schiller

In the fall of 2017, Ken Burns and Lynn Novick released *The Vietnam War* on PBS. My response to the film, episode after episode, scene after scene, interview after interview, was not how evil the war was, and certainly not what a "tragic mistake" it was, but how deadly *stupid* it all was. All the thoughtless truisms about halting the spread of communism, about domino theories, and about the loss of American prestige. Truisms about kill counts, and a war of attrition. Truisms about the American people, or American character, as if such things really existed. Truisms about duty and the flag, lugubrious Old Glory, and the importance of free markets, on which, for some reason, the flag should be draped. Truisms about our national interests, as revealed through Secretary McNamara's spreadsheets and analytics which, it's true, were good enough for the Ford assembly line back in Dearborn. Truisms about pacification. Truisms about hearts and minds. Truisms from the peak of Cold War paranoia: "Student opposition to the war was sponsored by Russia and

China!" said Lyndon Johnson, our first conspiracy-theorist-in-chief.

This is not to say that the people who believed these stories, or believe them still, were stupid, but that the stories themselves should have been seen as clearly stupid once inspected. No wonder that Abbie Hoffman and the Yippies *laughed* at what passed for intelligence within the political establishment of 1968. The Yippies mocked Wall Street, ran a pig for president, and levitated the Pentagon. They played the part of the crowd in "The Emperor's New Clothes": they *laughed* at the nakedness of these absurdities trying to pass for reasoned opinion and lawful authority. The Yippies were the children of Voltaire, who wrote, "I have never made but one prayer to God, a very short one: 'O Lord, make my enemies ridiculous.'"

Burns and Novick contend that talented people full of the best intentions made bad decisions that resulted in an "American tragedy" to which we must now be reconciled as a nation. This is the tendentious story they have to tell. Unfortunately, it is more accurate to say that *The Vietnam War* is a continuation of the stupidities that created the Vietnam War: our supposed intelligence, our mythic "good intentions," our deranged exceptionalism—all of that goes unquestioned. In fact, the film does yeoman's work reinforcing the ideology of the "American character," just as Burns has done in all of his PBS documentaries. There is this thing called "America," he says. It has a unique people and experience (PBS has a long-running series called *The American Experience*). It has a spirit. Even if it screws up now and then, it has the best intentions toward others. Revealingly, white nationalists like Richard Spencer think the same thing. As Spencer said at the 2017 Conservative Political Action Conference, "We have an organic nation, there is an American people that has a history, they have a particular experience." Burns agrees; he's just a little more inclusive about it, bless his liberal soul.

Such fictions are what William Blake meant by "mind-forged manacles." They are derivatives of patriotism, our founding intellectual crime. Sadly, it is through this originary crime that we have maintained a sense of ourselves as Americans. Our patriotic expressions serve the same tribal purpose as face paint—you know, "by these markers you shall know me." "I love my country," we say, marking ourselves as safe company for other patriots, and pity the fool who expresses misgivings.

I don't want to indulge in mere name-calling, so let me perform a short anatomy of stupidity, because it comes in different forms. There is, first, an elite form of stupidity that we might call "convenient stupidity." For instance, as a representative of American capitalism (the former president of Ford Motor Company) Secretary of Defense Robert McNamara was "conveniently stupid." In other words, it was in his self-interest to be stupid. He could say things like, "We seek an independent non-Communist South Vietnam . . . Unless we can achieve this objective almost all of Southeast Asia will probably fall under Communist dominance" . . . and here's a bar graph to prove it. This was a stupid thing to say, but it was also very convenient, or self-interested, for him and other members of the ruling class.

Another word for convenient stupidity is barbarity.

Joined to convenient stupidity in a disheartening dance of death is "sacrificial stupidity." Far and away the most common form of stupidity, the sacrificially stupid commit themselves to social fictions that tend to undermine their own most tangible interests. The jungles of Vietnam were full of young men who were sacrificially stupid. They thought their participation was about duty to country and the fight against communism, but what it was really about was accepting the empty risk of coming home in a box, or disabled, or so traumatized that they would spend the rest of their lives living on the street, in a tent, in downtown San Francisco. And Trump Nation couldn't exist without the sacrificially stupid. People voted for him believing that he would help "ordinary Americans," but they got a tax break for the already rich instead. The sacrificially stupid are the poster children of stupidity. There should be philanthropic foundations and ad campaigns for them.

Convenient stupidity may be sincere about the things it believes but maybe not. It could all be a con. But sacrificial stupidity is *sincere*. We think that people who have "sincere beliefs" should not be mocked. We assume that their sincerity is itself the mark of a kind of intelligence, or at least authenticity. But sincerity merely doubles down on stupidity. It is a way of saying, "I believe this thing. If you tell me that this thing I believe is stupid, never mind your 'evidence-based' reasons, there might be a fistfight." Sacrificial stupidity is one part loyalty to family and one part fear of the neighbors.

Beyond convenient and sacrificial stupidities, there is "inconvenient stupidity," that form of stupidity held by people who under ordinary circumstances would quite happily reside in their community's native stupidities (whether convenient or sacrificial) but who find that for the moment their native stupidities are such a gross existential threat that they must renounce them, no matter that said stupidities were taken at their mother's tit. This form of stupidity is in abundant display in *The Vietnam War* in the form of soldiers (John Musgrave), novelists (Tim O'Brien), journalists (Neil Sheehan), and politicians (William Fulbright), all of whom renounced their original support for the war and moved into the ranks of the anti-war movement.

The social and political dynamics of Vietnam were different in large part because so many people, especially the young, concluded that it was not at all convenient to be stupid but was instead, as any working-class person *should* have been able to tell them, greatly *inconvenient*, a real short-circuiting of expectations through jungle misery, trauma, mutilation, and death. That threat of death was crazy-making but also enlightening, even if only for the moment. The inconveniently stupid are like the grandmother in Flannery O'Connor's "A Good Man is Hard to Find." After shooting her, the murderous Misfit says, "She would have been a good woman if there had been someone there to shoot her every minute of her life."

But that moment of looking up the barrel of an NVA AK-47 passed and so too did the intelligence the barrel inspired. Nixon's creation of the draft lottery in 1969 and the end of the draft in 1973 meant, for a good two out of three draft-age boys, that they could "come home" to stupidity.* It was convenient once again to be stupid. The practical and sentimental "reasons to be stupid" were once again persuasive. The way was prepared for Jerry Rubin, most notoriously, and many others to join a renaissance on Wall Street in the go-go Reagan years. Free-market orthodoxy was given new vigor. An old stupidity in new garb had arrived: trickle down! Once

* *

* I still think that the draft lottery was the most brilliantly malign political move of the era. Psychologically astute. And effective.

again, the upper half of the country could reckon that someone might have to suffer for stupidity, but probably not them. Someone might have to suffer for military adventurism, but probably not them. Someone might have to suffer from the next stock bubble, but probably not them. Someone might have to suffer from environmental destruction, but probably not them, so they placed their bet on the system. Once again they had fair prospects of being able to join their families and communities in the pleasures capitalism offers its devotees, assured that the measure of their devotion to the Market God, the "God that Sucks," as Thomas Frank put it, would be measured back to them in cold cash. Stupidity was back on Easy Street! How convenient!

In spite of this familiar movement back to stupidity, some few of the inconveniently stupid actually became post-stupid (although I don't propose that as an official category). These few came to understand their inconvenient stupidity as something brand new that they called the Truth, to which they obstinately clung in spite of material and social self-interest. Such people became "transcendentally stupid" (that is a category, the fourth if you're paying attention). They were now stupid in the rarified sense that they "failed to understand what was obvious to everyone else," that is, they failed to understand all the deadly lazy, ho-hum cant of this American life. But the transcendentally stupid had a simpler word for their condition: they were *free*.

The transcendentally stupid are among us even now. Whether they are from privileged or working-class origins, the transcendentally stupid come to see the stories about God, country, and mammon as just so many tricks played on them to make them servile to the interests of the "one percent," as we say these days. The transcendentally stupid become class traitors, resistors, agitators, troublemakers, rebels, artists, dropouts, anarchists, and revolutionaries. Minority communities, especially African American communities, are forever skeptical of the "hype," and forever outside most state (if not religious) forms of sacrificial stupidity, for which Muhammad Ali's war resistance stands as a permanent marker deserving of a shrine in the National Mall. Ali was stupid in the sense that he failed to understand what was obvious to everyone else: patriotism. He said, "Why should they ask me to put on a uniform and go ten thousand miles from home and drop bombs and bullets on brown people in Vietnam while so-called Negro people in Louisville are treated like dogs?" Or as the hip-hop group Run the Jewels put it more recently, "Can't win no crown, holding what's holding you down."

That's transcendentally stupid. Take a knee!

Burns and Novick have no suggestions for what intelligence might have taken the place of the war's stupidities, never mind the fact that the possibilities were many and were everywhere during the war years. In particular, there is no consideration of culture in the film, and that in spite of the fact that "counterculture" is the most common media tag given to the period. Certainly Burns and Novick exploit the music of the era for their soundtrack, but there is no effort to explain or account for the role played by music, cinema, poetry, experimental fiction, and the visual arts, in shaping a response to the war.

Although the fact seems to be lost on Ken Burns, even a conservative commentator like David Brooks understands the centrality of culture to politics. In an eyebrow-raising column in 2017, he acknowledges that the large part of political debate in the United States is non-rational. Quoting Marilynne Robinson, Brooks asserts that our political conversations are more about "the pleasure of sharing an attitude one knows is socially approved." That is, people tend to retreat within the symbolic universes that are familiar to them. They retreat to what feels like family. These attitudes are approved within what C. S. Lewis called the Inner Ring, whether that Inner Ring is Harvard Square or the local VFW hall. This is more or less what we mean when we say that debate in social media is taking place in an "echo chamber": we hear only our own fond and familiar voices.

Brooks's contention is similar to what Nietzsche called "civic narcissism." This narcissism says, "Everyone should live through our ideals because our ideals are self-evidently the best. We're bewildered that others don't share our ideals, and we're indignant that these others are not persuaded when we loudly explain them. As a consequence, we would impose our ideals by main force if the opportunity presented itself. After all, it's in everyone's best interest."

In short, Brooks suggests, tribalism has gotten us into trouble, but "if social life can get us into trouble, social life can get us out." Brooks writes:

> After all, think of how you really persuade people. Do you do it by writing thoughtful essays that carefully marshal facts? That works some of the time. But the real way to persuade people is to create an attractive community that people want to join.[21]

Without intending to, Brooks succinctly describes the theory of counterculture, the un-thought thought behind much of the art of the '60s. That art, that culture, that social experiment, was very much a part of the war in Vietnam. It sought to create a reality separate from the reality that wagged a beckoning, bloody finger from the jungles of Southeast Asia. It offered pleasure, color, freedom, and play, and said, "Really, wouldn't you rather live here?" Literally, *here* in one hippy refuge or another—the Haight or Telegraph Avenue; Taos or Athens, Georgia; Homer, Alaska or Port Townsend, Washington.

Of course, David Brooks has none of this in mind. His counter-communities have a familiar look: family, church, entrepreneurial capitalism, and, in this column, the Yale Political Union. In other words, his resistant communities tend to have a family resemblance to the Inner Ring of American oligarchy.

An argument similar to Brooks's comes from a more likely source, writer and activist George Monbiot's "The Power of Stories." Monbiot argues:

> When we encounter a complex issue and try to understand it, what we look for is not consistent and reliable facts but a consistent and comprehensible story . . . A string of facts, however well attested, has no power to correct or dislodge a powerful story. The only response it is likely to provoke is indignation: people often angrily deny facts that clash with the narrative "truth" established in their minds. The only thing that can displace a story is a story.[22]

Joining Monbiot's argument to Brooks's, we can say that what makes communities are their stories. In short, *if we want new communities, we have to provide new stories for people to live through*—precisely the role of the counterculture in the '60s. And so we can say that Ken Burns is a storyteller, but it would be more accurate to say that he is a story-repeater—in other words, an ideologue. *The Vietnam War* nominates no characters beyond the usual suspects: the great men—the senators and generals—and the great events—the battles and political campaigns. The story that Burns and Novick repeat basically has to do with the legitimacy of the ruling class decision-makers to make the decisions they made and, worse yet, the legitimacy of those decision-makers to make future decisions, chastened, Burns hopes, by the errors of the past. But what if those errors were in fact an acknowledgment of the ruling class's essence? The Vietnam War was not a mistake running against the American spirit; it was a confession of that spirit's essence. We did not need to be protected from communism; we needed to be protected from social elites who claimed to be protecting us from communism.

Tell that story. It's still *the point*.

We need much more than what Burns and Novick have to offer. In fact, we need resistance to their stories through counter-stories and counter-communities speaking in the name of and in the spirit of alternative worlds, possible worlds. We need to become transcendentally stupid because transcendental stupidity is not only stupid to what others think is true; it is also *stupid about what others assume to be impossible*: a more equal and just world, a world given to *life*, beyond techno-capitalism, beyond neo-liberalism. In short, we need countercultures, whether you label them communism, communes, counter-community, regular community, neighborhood, or what-you-will.

But first we need the counter-stories. And what will they look like, these stories? Well, perhaps they will look like this book, the book in your hands. Because I am, I admit, telling you a story.

This digression may seem to you not only impertinent but also intemperate. Perhaps it will seem to you only a rant, something that should be dismissed by more sober or "realistic" reflection. Ken Burns, you say, is not the problem. He loves America, or the idea of America, just as many of us do. He likes baseball and national parks. Why pick on him?

Perhaps this is so. But impertinent or not, intemperate or not, anti-American or not, if we are ever to escape the centripetal pull of our many inherited delusions, our "collective shadow," that lead us from one disaster to the next and leave us confused and wondering "where we went wrong," then just this sort of unremitting honesty, this impertinence, is a *requirement*.

PART
IV

A mile wide *an an inch deep*

COUNTERCULTURE IS
IMPROVISATIONAL

The efforts of our varied political camps to create a national "we the people" have had the opposite effect: they have created a war of all-against-all in which "my countrymen are my enemy." That short sentence by James Baldwin brings us about as close to national reality as a sentence can.

In spite of that robust fact, most socialists still imagine that their primary objective is to create a "mass movement" in which some badly understood "we" emerges triumphant. Unfortunately, that is a vain and potentially bloody fantasy. No mass movement is alone and triumphant. There are always others, other masses.

Any nationwide reordering of values accomplished by either the Left (supporters of Bernie Sanders, socialists to one degree or another) or the Right (the Tea Party, evangelicals, the Alt-Right) will be bloody, or, less theatrically, an expression of force. The Right gets that—enthusiastically, as the Rise Above movement of fascist "serial rioters" has demonstrated—and is locked and loaded.* When the Bundy clan seized a federal building in eastern Oregon, there were few other human beings for hundreds of miles around, but the watchtower was manned, and the windows were hispid with rifles.

. . . .

* As Rise Above member Benjamin Drake Daley gleefully exclaimed on Facebook, "I hit like five people." Dude!

More ominously, Texas is as close as a state can come to living in permanent preparedness for war with its own government, both in principle and in fact, as we saw in 2015 when Governor Greg Abbott activated the Texas State Guard to monitor the U.S. Army's Jade Helm 15 military training exercises in southwest Texas. Of course, Abbott's actions were redundant. Virtually the whole of rural Texas is one vast citizen's militia, one great *posse comitatus*. (Was Abbott perhaps trying to protect the Army from the Texans?)

In pristine terms, as Trump supporter Steve Spaeth of West Bend, Wisconsin, said to his liberal sister, "If there is a civil war in this country and you were on the wrong side, I would have no problem shooting you in the face." Not just shoot her, mind you, but shoot her *in the face*. There is something perversely aspirational about his violent fantasy. It is also close to a confession about what the Right is, deep in its malign heart.[23]

And what the Left is *not*.

And yet if the Left is to have anything remotely like what it says it wants, it will have to fight, something it seems mostly disinclined to do. You can hardly blame them (and by them I mean me). We think that in a democracy issues should be decided in the favor of whoever offers the best reasons. Good luck with that. When *The New York Times* ran a front-page editorial articulating the reasons for its support of gun control, right-wing commentator Erick Erickson forsook rebuttal and shot the page full of holes.

In contrast, counterculture resists not through new state institutions or by threatening blood but by offering a cultivated disinterest. It doesn't say, "J'accuse," it says, "Je refuse," or, as Herman Melville's Bartleby the Scrivener said, "I would prefer not to." This refusal is cultivated in the sense that it well understands the basis of social antagonism, and can articulate its own critique of it, is even willing to throw its weight into political action when it can, but in the end it understands that it has more important things to do. It understands that destruction is not something threatening us from the future, destruction is the way we live now, and so we need to live differently *now* and not when the "glittering hopes" of socialism are realized. We don't have the luxury of waiting for the time when the Green New Deal is universally embraced, or when capitalism sees the wisdom of universal employment and the twenty-hour workweek, or when we persuade our conservative antagonists to see things our way.

No one speaks of the politics of refusal as a legitimate political strategy these days, and yet our history contains many powerful examples of it. We know it through Marx's son-in-law Paul Lafargue's *The Right To Be Lazy* (as opposed to the "right to work" ideology still inflicted upon workers).* We know it through Thoreau's "disobedience" and *Walden*, and through Tolstoy. As he writes in his novella *Family Happiness* (1859):

> A quiet secluded life in the country, with the possibility of being useful to people to whom it is easy to do good, and who are not accustomed to have it done to them; then work which one hopes may be of some use; then rest, nature, books, music, love for one's neighbor—such is my idea of happiness.

* For contemporary versions of Lafargue's idea, see Bob Black's *The Abolition of Work* (1985) ("I call for a collective adventure in generalized joy and freely interdependent exuberance"), or Pat Kane's *The Play Ethic: A Manifesto For a Different Way of Living* (2005), or Jenny Odell's *How to Do Nothing: Resisting the Attention Economy* (2019).

Much more recently, we know it through the hippy (re)invention of the commune, through refusal of the military draft (remember draft card burning?), and we know it through punk's exclamatory version of rock and its DIY squatters' communities of the 1980s in New York's Lower East Side. The "not in my name" response to George W. Bush's invasion of Iraq had the flavor of refusal, and so does the Trump hashtag "not my president." Occupy Wall Street's Zuccotti Park encampment was a tangible refusal of what the rest of us thought was simply reality. Occupy's work is best understood not just as a set of demands to be satisfied through legislative reform, and still less through a political revolution, but as a performance, a presentation of itself as an alternative way of living now.

Far from dying away with the '60s, counterculture's music (psychedelia, New Wave, and now "indie") exploded in the late '70s and '80s giving us space to breathe (and room to move) as Apple and Amazon's techno-tsunami progressed. Sonic Youth, Pixies, Elvis Costello, and Nina Hagen made the '80s "lively up." Radiohead, Björk, and the Elephant Six bands of Athens, Georgia (of Montreal, Olivia Tremor Control, and Neutral Milk Hotel) were not far behind. Most recently, groups like the Ty Segall Band, Parquet Courts, and Deerhunter have all been enlivened by Pete Townshend's cry, "I'm free!" For decades now even the most debt-ridden, discouraged, and alienated have found solace, inspiration, and refuge in this music.

Countercultural literature is not only still alive but enormously expanded through the small-press movement begun by Beat publishers like City Lights and Black Sparrow and greatly enlarged in the '70s and '80s by avant-literary presses: the Fiction Collective (first publisher of Russell Banks and Mark Leyner), Douglas Messerli's

Sun and Moon (first publisher of Paul Auster), John O'Brien's Dalkey Archive Press (Gilbert Sorrentino, Ishmael Reed, Rikki Ducornet), as well as Copper Canyon, Graywolf, Coffee House Press, and FC2, most of these still very much alive and at work. The list is growing through the efforts of Debra Di Blasi's Jaded Ibis Press, Two Dollar Radio, and, as the book in your hand shows, Melville House Publishing.

In a more down-to-earth mode, community agriculture continues to refuse industrial agriculture practices through farmers' markets, grocery co-ops, farm-to-fork programs, and meat and egg production that at least tries to limit the process's innate cruelty. The "local" movement in food does not wait until factory farming has been regulated out of existence by an enlightened central government. Community agriculture implements the world it wants right *now*, complete with a Saturday market, tables full of pottery and handmade jewelry, and a local bluegrass band. (At the Saturday market here in Port Townsend, a musician plays a cello over his knee like a Stratocaster, toggling between Bach and Keith Richards.) This is the work of culture and of creativity. More to the point, it is the gift of '60s counterculture, the triumph of that counterculture, alive and well today.*

My point with this partial inventory of refusenik glories is that *we don't have to start from scratch*. And that is such good news. These political, musical, literary, and agricultural movements, these *countercultures*, are the work of democratic improvisation, as are the thousands of Buddhist *sanghas* flourishing across the country.

. . . .

* See Jonathan Kauffman's *Hippie Food: How Back-to-the-Landers, Longhairs, and Revolutionaries Changed the Way We Eat* (2018).

As Bob Marley sang, "Lively up yourself! Come alive today!"

Earlier I suggested that countercultures present and future are about "socialist survivalism," a necessary thing in the context of climate change and geopolitical terror (the Bulletin of Atomic Scientists reports that in 2018 we were two minutes from nuclear midnight). But I think it might be more truthful, and certainly more appealing, to say that countercultures led by art, music, books, rich gardens, and local democracy are really about "sustainable happiness," Tolstoy's happiness. The fake happiness provided by the anomie and isolation of smartphones—or by a Tesla, or a brimming bank account, or a hundred bicycles—is the happiness offered to us by the money regime, by our dying conviction that money is the universal value. But that is a lie: "There is no wealth but life," as John Ruskin insisted. And that is what counterculture understands best.

Obviously, this wealth is present now, but it is constrained and fragmented. There is not enough awareness that these fragments—the arts, the garden, the politics of refusal—could be joined more consciously, more productively, and more forcefully in new forms of community. Counterculture has its silos too, unfortunately. An understanding of an integrated and, therefore, fully living culture is lacking . . . but not far away.

In a 2015 essay in *The New York Times* Kevin Baker argued that American democracy works best when it is not driven by representatives faithfully mirroring the will of constituents. It works best when parties are fragmented and politicians have no choice but to stitch together majorities from inter-party coalitions. For Baker, this "practical democracy" has an enviable record for progressive reform, including labor law, social security, minority rights, etc. For instance, the Voting Rights Act of 1965 was signed by a Democratic president over the objections of southern Democrats and with the support of moderate Republicans.[24]

In an era of hyper-partisanship, Baker's ideal has appeal, even though it ignores the outsized influence of concentrated wealth on all factions. His "practical democracy" is merely collusion if the two parties are just arms of the one great Party of Business, as they are. Perhaps what he is saying is that democracy works best when it is not working democratically. Which is to suggest that the very idea of democracy is an empty talisman, a sort of gilded idol, behind which there are only myths and legends, piety, and the fear that if the fiction of democracy no longer stabilizes social discourse, some worse barbarity will take its place. This is not an unreasonable fear, as the Alt-Right, the Proud Boys, and that enfant terrible of fascist haute couture, Milo Yiannopoulos, have flamboyantly shown.

What's missing in Baker's pragmatic rendering of political life in Washington is any suggestion that a similarly non-ideological pragmatism might succeed back home as well. Why should communities, cities, and states wait for centralized deal-making to get things done, especially when that deal-making always seems to benefit the wealthy first? After all, people have been making their own deals by voting with their feet for the last half century, moving to whatever part of the country seemed most welcoming to them. The consequences of this nomad democracy are important and familiar—that is, we are already on a family footing with these consequences. The trend is obvious, if not well understood, so let's go a little deeper.

m.6

The path our feet have followed was pioneered in the 1960s when gay men from all over the country began moving to the Castro District in San Francisco. What the gay community was creating was not just a safe place for gays to be who they were but a new form of democratic action, an improvisatory democracy beyond democracy. If the nation could not give them justice, they would provide it for themselves by creating communities and cultures that countered the communities and cultures they had the misfortune to be born into, thus the worthy sanctification of leaders like Harvey Milk.

More recently, our nomad democracy has been deepened through the legalization of marijuana in Washington, Colorado, and now California. Unless the federal government has a change of heart, it is now okay for some states to be federal scofflaws. Add to that the "Fight for $15" minimum wage laws and the growth of worker cooperatives in California and Seattle. As Nathan Schneider writes in his recent book, *Everything For Everyone: The Radical Tradition That is Shaping the Next Economy*: "This book is a sojourn among the frontiers of cooperation, past and present . . . It's about the long history and present revival of an economy in which people can own and govern the businesses where they work, shop, bank, or meet, sharing the risk and the rewards."[25]

Add to this the sanctuary city movement. Add to the sanctuary movement transgender rights legislation. Add to all of that state and local protection of the environment (as with California's aggressive CAFE standards) and progressive funding of recreation. Health care, too, is becoming an odd sort of state's rights issue: in

San Francisco, the Healthy SF program mandates employer contributions to health care for restaurant workers.*

Go to a gun show in Texas; go to a coffee shop in Portland—they're different countries. Soon, we'll be talking not about states rights but about autonomous regions. A regime of supportive tolerance for such territorial differences should create, in time, ever-finer fragmentations of culture within progressive regions, assuming that people feel free to self-invent and assuming a prevailing atmosphere of benevolence.

As for those dancing to the Red State Blues, perhaps even NRA types might be more benevolent and tolerant of difference if they did not feel they were being coerced by government, by the North, by elites, by those they think of as socialists. Eventually, as the mass shootings in suburban and rural areas pile up—Benton, Kentucky, a school cafeteria outside Dallas, a school bus in rural Iowa, Wake Forest University in North Carolina, all in the same grim week in the winter of 2017, accelerating in succeeding years, including a border patrol agent turned serial killer in 2018 and, of course, the Parkland massacre—the pro-gun people of the South will have to do some soul searching. If they're not capable of this soul searching, as far as I'm concerned, they're welcome to their misery.

That may sound callous, as if I'm abandoning the people of

- -

* Of course, the billionaire owners of the restaurants are pushing back some. As Tilman Fertitta, star of CNBC's "Billion Dollar Buyer" and owner of Rainforest Café, has wearily observed, "All these states now are doing their own mandates. Why should the city of San Francisco be able to do absolutely whatever they want to do?" (Alyssa Pereira, "Billionaire behind Rainforest Café, Bubba Gump's: 'We can't afford'" to give SF worker healthcare," *SFGate*, March 8, 2017)

rural America and the South who want equality, health care, and gun control, but this is part of what it means to say "it can't be fixed." We can't fix the South's affection for guns, their hypocritical version of Christianity, or their obsession with race. Of course, for most Southerners, the idea that there is anything about their culture that needs fixing is an outrage. If there's fixin' to be done, they'll do it themselves. And in truth the South can't be fixed by anyone other than Southerners. Those who try will be cordially hated for their efforts, efforts which are likely to lead to hyperbolically unintended consequences, as with the election of an orange-haired reality show billionaire president.

Progressive regionalism need not be merely a matter of making the best of a broken situation. It can be a virtue, a virtue of *place*. The American architect Christopher Alexander imagines both nation and cities as "mosaics of subcultures" which foster both a strong sense of personal identity and a freedom to move among subcultures. For regions, he writes, "independent regions are the natural receptacles for language, culture, customs, economy, and laws" and "each region should be separate and independent enough to maintain the strength and vigor of its culture."[26]

the end of America

And for cities:

> In a city made of a large number of subcultures relatively small in size, each occupying an identifiable place and separated from other subcultures by a boundary of nonresidential land, new ways of life can develop. People can choose the kind of subculture they wish to live in, and can still experience many

ways of life different from their own. Since each environment fosters mutual support and a strong sense of shared values, individuals can grow.[27]

This is a great improvement over Kevin Baker's formulation because it decentralizes authority and makes the places where people live the site of ongoing self-creation. Even so, there are problems with this separatist logic in present circumstances. One obvious problem is the red, white, and blue gorilla in the room, the North American nation-state, the good old U. S. of A.

As the poet-biologist Lewis Thomas memorably put it, the modern nation-state is "the most stupefying example of biological error since the age of the great reptiles, wrong at every turn, but always felicitating itself loudly on its great value."[28] * That problem—the problem that is daily fodder for Fox News, MSNBC, and *The New York Times*—is not going away, and the need to find ways of responding to it is not going away either. We ignore our disunited and increasingly fascistic nation at our peril. Nevertheless, this is exactly the world that can't be fixed. If all of our energies go into resisting it, or trying to replace it, or treating it as an obsessive or addictive spectator sport (as Fox and MSNBC do), we are without hope. We become mere figures in something like Pieter Bruegel the Elder's vast *Triumph of Death* (1562), where the hope of human happiness is merely something to mock (a skeleton playing a hurdy-gurdy, as if to say, "You thought life could be about music?!").

* *

* "I don't dream about the President any more, and when I talk to my friends, I find they don't either. The Great Leader is a hollow man, the Law of the Market cannot prove itself, and the Nation State mocks its own values" Robert Aitken, *The Mind of Clover* (1984).

Let me emphasize this point, because I don't want it to seem that my call for reimagined countercultures means that national politics can be ignored. But we don't want to be misled by those offering false hopes that the political system can be transformed to our satisfaction anytime soon. It can only be moved by inches (although there are times when those inches are precious). What I am suggesting is a better proportioning of our energies, so that more of our energy goes toward creating life rather than merely reacting to the next turn of the national political screw (and it can always get a little tighter).

Italians have a useful way of articulating this proportion. The phrase *mio paese* (my country) means first for them not the nation but the community in which they were born—Padua, Sienna—to which they owe love and communal care. The Italian republic is an ephemeral thing (sixty-one governments since the end of World War II), but the city-state is still a powerful part of the Italian psyche, surviving through *campanilismo*: every Italian knows the sound of the bell tower, the *campanile*, in their town. It is the sound of home.

We think that the Italian nation is to be pitied for its political instability; they think we are to be pitied for the poverty of our *comune*, the lives we share in common in the places where we actually live. With a future made ever more unpredictable by climate change, sectarian violence, and economic inequality, we need to think of the places where we live, rather than the nation that we mostly endure, as a primary if not exclusive focus for our work. We need a renewal of the idea of Home, or, int he words of Theodore Roszak at least "something a human being can identify as home."

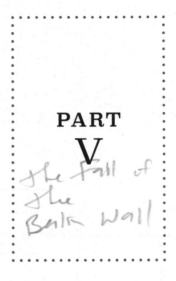

PART

V

the fall of
the
Berlin Wall

THE COUNTER-
COUNTERCULTURE

"The problem is this: How to love people who have no use."
—Kurt Vonnegut, *God Bless You, Mr. Rosewater*

The nation-state is not the only "gorilla in the room." Standing next to it is a gorilla in a human suit: capitalism and its money system. Think of the money system as an electrical circuit. Money flows. We believe, and not without reason, that we will not be allowed to live without our own little node on the money circuit through which money flows to our bank accounts, is siphoned off to student loans and credit card debt, puddles pathetically in savings, and wrecks nerves and causes nightmares of sleeping in a broke-down RV in the Sodo district of Seattle. So there's that little difficulty. But there's something more, and more insidious, because oddly enough we enjoy the money system; we like the "place" it provides for us, or we think we do. Our bank accounts may be a node on an enslaving money circuit, but . . . isn't it pleasant?

I came across a phrase recently that made me pause: the "comforts of *samsara*." *Samsara* is the Buddhist word for the world we live in, the world of "suffering and change." I had always imagined that this suffering was about universal and inevitable things like sickness, death, cruelty, anger, and greed. So, what could the *comforts* of *samsara* mean? It's an oxymoron: "The comforts of suffering."

It means that there are damaging consequences for the things

that we think we most need and enjoy: a house full of agreeable
things, the comfort of meat, the comfort of free home delivery, the
pleasures of a fully loaded sedan, or of a Ram-tough truck—best in
class, top customer loyalty—and package deals to vacation hotspots,
all inclusive! It's the "bourgeois art of life" (Roland Barthes), and it
is as comforting as it is destructive.

Here's a trivial personal example: I recently purchased a set of
Sony wireless headphones. Would I have been deprived of the pleasures of music without them? Hardly, though I won't go into any
embarrassing details about my audiophile rig. But there can always
be a *little more* music, right?

Was I aware of the social and environmental costs of buying
these "cans," buying them along with millions of other people all
over the blessed world, nodding their heads to the beat, all convinced that they are a wonderful thing? Was I aware that "plastic is
forever"? Was I aware of the working conditions for people who as-
semble these products? Was I aware of the "carbon footprint" that I
purchased along with the headphones? The manufacture, the shipping, the car trip to the store to purchase, the landfill to which they
will eventually be consigned?

Yeah, I was aware, but boy do they sound great! Besides, it was
a birthday present. Surely that excuses something. But I'm whim-
pering, and, as T. S. Eliot observed, that's the way the world ends,
not with a bang but a whimper.

In spite of our capture in the capitalist money system, advocates
of progressive autonomous regions (it's "Cascadia" out here on the
Left Coast) continue to imagine that one of the primary movers
of this regional autonomy will be progressive good-citizen corporations, especially in the tech sector. Of course, these corporations

have encouraged this perception. As Google has said of itself, "Don't be evil." And Apple, "Think different." And Amazon, "Work hard. Have fun. Make history."

Unfortunately, this is a delusion because capitalism—even socially enlightened techno-capitalism—does not have what theologian Paul Tillich called an "ultimate concern" other than whatever serves the private interests of the moment, as Amazon has proven in its appalling self-dealing with New York's HQ2—"Have fun!" Amazon may ally itself with progressive forces when it is in its interest to do so, but it will also make itself regressive, as Amazon has, when it is in its interest to do so— as when it opposed Seattle's employee head tax intended to help pay for housing for the homeless. Not only does Amazon in particular and capitalism in general not want to pay a tax on the people it employs, *it would like not to have those employees at all*, or certainly fewer of them, as few as possible, for the simple and very old-fashioned reason that labor costs drive down profits.

Capitalism has always been in the business of trying to rid itself of its dependence on labor, which is to say, its dependence on people. Capitalism sees the power of labor unions as a defeat visited upon it by the New Deal, and it is not finished reversing that fact, as "right to work" legislation, bankrolled by the Koch brothers and others, continues to demonstrate.* Worse yet, this war against labor has become a sort of generalized war against people, and the

. . . .

* As I wrote this, the "Janus Case" (*Janus v. American Federation of State, County and Municipal Employees, Council 31*) was decided by the Supreme Court in favor of Janus and, implicitly, free market capitalism. Presented as a workers' rights issue, the suit was supported by Grover Norquist's American Legislative Exchange Council, the Koch brothers' Americans for Prosperity, and the union-busting State Policy Network (sponsor of the Goldwater Institute).

proof of this is the enormous "surplus population," the population of people who are unneeded, or feel unneeded, because they are being used in some less-than-fulfilling way.

Psychologically, the "unneeded" are up and down the income spectrum: from richly compensated data droids, to precarious baristas with advanced degrees in sociology, to supermarket cashiers and taxi drivers waiting for the robot ax to fall, to new-styled "contract workers" in the gig economy (Uber, etc.), and, of course, the multitude of the under- and unemployed bobbing in the dead man's float in the penumbra of the service economy. They all feel in their slowly sinking hearts a little or a lot superfluous.

To be sure, there will still be workers because someone will have to keep the robots in working order, a few people will be needed to clap at the year-end rituals of self-congratulation that billionaire philanthropists will create for themselves, basking narcissistically in "all the good we do," and someone will have to buy the "crappy shit" (Marx) that the robots produce, even if that requires handing out guaranteed minimum incomes to the idle.

Consider this dystopian vision. We get the Guaranteed Minimum Income we're all supposed to want, and the economy then looks like this: the oligarchs take the profits through prodigious monopoly rents; robots do most of the work; the world is awash with cheap consumer goods; and we superseded humans have the privilege of paying for those goods with free money. This will be not just an economic circle jerk but a vicious economic circle jerk. (Required re-reading: Kurt Vonnegut's *Player Piano*.)

But beyond that we know their oligarchic preference: they'd prefer there were fewer of us, a lot fewer of us. As more job categories go to robots, ever more of the freshly available capital goes into developing AI.* The oligarchs don't mind conversing with Alexa and Siri—it's a lot better than talking to labor lawyers (speaking of doomed employment categories)—and, with VR porn and sexbots just around the corner, there'll be no need to sexually harass the junior execs, secretarial staff, and nubile post-grad interns. Just ask Andy Puzder, CEO of Carl's Jr. and one-time Trump nominee for secretary of labor, "[Robots are] always polite, they always upsell, they never take a vacation, they never show up late, there's never a slip-and-fall, or an age, sex, or race discrimination case."[29]

Given this antipathy to humans, do you think that in their heart of hearts the oligarchs care if climate change brings about a human population crash? Or is that merely the ultimate term of Wall Street's mantra, "When there's blood in the street, there's money to be made"?† Oligarchs work from the assumption that they will be among the survivors of any population crash; they work from the assumption that it is *our* blood that's at stake. The long 2019 federal government shutdown illustrated this clearly enough. Eight hundred thousand furloughed workers struggled to

. . . .

* On cue, in October 2018, MIT announced that it is investing $1 billion, including $350 million from the Blackstone Group, the giant private equity firm, to create a "College of Computing." The purpose of the college will be to "educate the bilinguals of the future." By "bilingual" MIT means that it plans to make computing and AI part of the skill set of *every* academic discipline, including psychotherapy: the Woebot, your chatbot mental health therapist, can see you now.

† The idea that climate change offers investment opportunities has already been embraced by Deutsche Bank's $2.9 billion DWS Climate Change Fund. In public statements the bank has reasoned, "Without taking a position on climate change, DWS Climate Change Fund is on the cutting edge of climate change investing." (See McKenzie Funk's *Windfall: the Booming Business of Global Warming* (2014).)

pay rent and eat while the Trump millionaires cabinet suggested, in the words of his daughter-in-law Lara Trump, "It's a little bit of pain, but it's going to be for the future of our country," thus implying that federal workers were not only poor but stupid.

So, do the oligarchs care if there are millions fewer people around the country, or billions fewer people around the globe? No, because they long ago concluded that those humans were not needed anyway and that money insulates them from having to suffer along with these "throwaway humans." In other words, the oligarchic assumption is that if you have enough money, you can escape.[30]

Of course, avoiding the unhappy fate of "surplus populations" is not the only reason the super-rich have for wanting to escape. There is also the very real possibility that climate collapse will take the financial system with it, presenting this novel problem: "How do I remain rich even after the end of money and a habitable planet?"

Perhaps you think that a ridiculous question. I do. But apparently there are people out there taking it very seriously. Some people imagine that hyper-money, cryptocurrencies like Bitcoin, will be needed after the end of the world. For the world's economic centers, global mega-cities like San Francisco and Shenzhen, this "shadow money" is the new inevitable. (And so, inevitably, in February 2019, JPMorgan Chase became the first major U.S. bank to introduce its own digital token for real-world use.)[31] Cryptocurrencies will allow wealthy individuals to create their own techno-libertarian paradises in Puerto Rico, New Zealand, and other global outposts where a Randian "cognitive elite" will design a new dispensation for the privileged alone.

An article in *The New York Times* in February 2018 provided the first glimpse of this "fundamentally new society": a group of cryptocurrency billionaires descended upon the ruins of hapless Puerto Rico, took over the twenty-thousand-square-foot Monastery Hotel, and announced its intention to create Puertopia. As Brock Pierce, the messianic leader of this group, articulated his vision, "If you take the MY out of money, you're left with ONE." Crypto investor Kai Nygard said of Pierce, "He's tuned in to a higher calling. He's beyond money." He is also, apparently, beyond irony because cryptocurrencies like Bitcoin are increasingly suspect for the wasteful use of electricity in cryptocurrency "mining," thus driving forward the climate crisis that virtual money is supposed to protect them from. Worse yet, schemes like Puertopia leave out most women investors and engineers who look in on these cyber utopias only to see the same old con: "blockchain bros." At the North American Bitcoin Conference in January 2018, the official conference party was held at a Miami strip club.[32]

And if cyber utopias don't work, what's left? Why, they'll just have to leave the planet! As Douglas Rushkoff explains,

[The techno-rich are] preparing for a digital future that has a whole lot less to do with making the world a better place than it does with transcending the human condition altogether and insulating themselves from a very real and present danger of climate change, rising sea levels, mass migrations, global pandemics, nativist panic, and resource depletion. For them, the future of technology is really about just one thing: escape.[33]

If the Elon Musks of the world have their way, that escape will be quite literal: the rich will achieve escape velocity! In the week of

December 17, 2018, SpaceX, Arianespace, Blue Origin, and United Launch Alliance all scheduled rocket launches. Musk's SpaceX expects an unpiloted trip to Mars in 2022 and a crewed flight to follow in 2024.

All right! Mars it is! Who's in!?

As for the rest of us, it will not only be Kazakhstan's saiga antelopes that will die in the tens of thousands in mass mortality events. Millions of humans are at risk of joining them belly-up on the plains. According to the 2018 Global Climate Risk Index, the nine countries most affected by climate change in the past twenty years are developing nations, including Honduras, Haiti, Burma, Pakistan, and Bangladesh. In Central America, tens of thousands of laborers have died from chronic kidney disease (CKD) with a strong correlation to an increase in solar radiation and heat waves. In Nicaragua, approximately 75 percent of the deaths among young and middle-aged men are attributed to CKD. One Nicaraguan town has been dubbed *"La isla de viudas,"* the "island of widows."[34] And in Cape Town, South Africa, "Day Zero" is coming—no water—but that doesn't make mammoth droughts a priority for the EPA or anybody else. It's industrial-strength genocide on a global scale. It's eco-apartheid. The oligarchs feel no compunctions about this because, as Thomas Malthus put it in *An Essay on the Principle of Population* (1803), the poor man "has no business to be where he is. At nature's mighty feast there is no vacant cover for him. She tells him to be gone, and will quickly execute her own orders."

Or as Orson Welles's Harry Lime put it, looking down on the "suckers" from his Vienna Ferris wheel in *The Third Man*:

Would you really feel any pity if one of those dots stopped moving forever? If I offered you twenty thousand pounds for every dot that stopped, would you really, old man, tell me to keep my money, or would you calculate how many dots you could afford to spare? Free of income tax, old man. Free of income tax—the only way you can save money nowadays.

Apparently, the answer to Lime's question is millions. Millions of dots, billions!

While the oligarchs patiently await their techno-rapture to Mars, they still think that if there were fewer of us, they could keep the place a little neater, a little shinier. They're already busy with this housework through "anti-homeless architecture" in Seattle, San Francisco, London, and Cologne. Business districts now shine with artful "unpleasant designs" (Selena Savić) for discouraging tents, sleeping bags, and generally any body at rest: elegant spikes on the sidewalk, graceful but uncomfortable ridges on benches, tents displaced by bike racks where there are no bikes, and hydrophobic paint on walls that splashes urine back on the urinator. And in Los Angeles's Industrial District, the "North Sea beautification program" has fenced off sidewalks from the homeless in order to create "a self-funded, beautification program involving thematic murals, sidewalk landscaping, a variety of sculptural interventions, and lots and lots of elbow grease. Our mission is to restore a sense of place and community pride." Now, that is some audacious spin!

As Louis XIV put it when he was condemning someone to death, "He is someone we do not know." Our oligarchs say, "He is someone we do not see." If, unlike Louis XIV, the oligarchs can't kill the homeless and the poor, or can't kill them overtly, and if the homeless don't have the good sense to crawl off and die on their own accord, at least keep them moving, preferably somewhere out of sight.

This is important for economic as well as aesthetic reasons, as we saw writ large with Amazon's quest for HQ2 in 2017. Cities compete with each other for businesses, so they try to be careful about their "brand." San Francisco has enjoyed immense branding advantages because of the "symbolic capital" provided by its location, its culture, and its reputation as a tech hotspot. Even so, homeless encampments, human feces, and piles of hypodermic needles in the Tenderloin affect San Francisco's brand, something the new African American mayor, the enviably named London Breed, has promised to fix. This is an even bigger problem for homicide capitals like Baltimore, Detroit, and the South Side of Chicago. As with any fascist state, cities don't want the "lesser sorts," the "*untermenschen*," hanging around sullying the brand. They don't have state anthropologists measuring skulls and enforcing sterilization, but that doesn't mean they're not serious about keeping the place clean (if not cleansed).

But it's not just the homeless and poor that the oligarchs want out of sight, it's not just the homeless that they "don't know": it's you, it's your modest home, it's your tacky town, and your "shithole" state. In fact, excluding a few national parks needed for vacay photo ops, it's the vast interior of the country, starting in Fresno and stretching to Newark.

The oligarchs and their minions don't have to be evil to proceed in these ways, and they don't have to be cruel. In fact, they can feel quite innocent, as innocent as any life form, beginning with bacteria, that moves forward directed by its own life force, its sense of its own pleasures. *They all, oligarch and bacteria alike, want the perfection of any world that is premised upon their own success.*

After all, it's not as if the oligarchs set out to harm large masses of other people. They are as surprised as anyone that the innocent, even meritorious, pursuit of their own prosperous interests and pleasures has these catastrophic consequences for others. And yet, some secret part of themselves also believes—maybe guiltily, maybe not—that there is truth in the idea that many of these people were a problem requiring a solution anyway. Or as Harry Lime put it, "The dead are better off dead, old boy," especially if they have died to make way for a more perfect union of wealth and a very cold beauty. The appropriate logo for a world watched over by money and machines, the World as Brand, is the flamethrower made by Elon Musk's Boring Company.

French philosopher Jean Baudrillard had it right in 1986 when he wrote:

> Entire social groups are being laid waste from the inside (individuals too). Society has forgotten them and now they are forgetting themselves . . . The social order is contracting to include only economic exchange, technology, the sophisticated and innovative; as it intensifies these sectors, entire zones are "disintensified," becoming reservations, and sometimes not even that: dumping grounds, wastelands, new deserts for the new poor, like the deserts you see forming around nuclear power stations or motorways.[35]

If you think that this sort of rhetoric is inflated, some critics are already claiming that San Francisco is a gated community and no longer a city. That story is told in ringing tones in Alexandra Pelosi's documentary *San Francisco 2.0* (2015). Pelosi asks two questions: How do the dot-com corporations and startups understand what they are doing in San Francisco and the South Bay? And how do the longtime residents of San Francisco experience the city's new techie residents? Then she lets people talk.

The youngsters ("tech bros") in the employ of the tech industry are not unsympathetic figures. They're smart, excited about what they're doing, and just as open to new ideas as they are reputed to be. You'd say that there is something anarchistic about them if it weren't anarchism swimming in comforting pools of venture capital. They are by all appearances having fun, enjoying both their work and each other, and they are really, really detached from what their presence means for the people living in a city with its own important history. Pelosi's film reveals them as charming and bright but lacking in sympathetic imagination—the ability to imagine what it's like to be someone else, someone other than their own personal bright and shiny selves.

The techies live in a youth bubble. It is implausible to them that the "old people" they are replacing were once the artists, the poets, the bohemians, and generally, as Steve Jobs put it, the "different" who made San Francisco wonderful in the second half of the last century. Their arrival in San Francisco, now a weird sort of bedroom suburb for Silicon Valley, makes literal the old Firesign Theater joke about the Trail of Tears Golf Course: "This is a line of Indians leaving Rancho Malario. To make room for *you!*"

And yet when the techies are confronted with these criticisms, they seem mostly impatient, as if they don't see quite why they should be bothered about local issues when they have more important things to do, things that Steve Jobs understood better than anyone before or since: they are making people rich, and they are "creating the future." Isn't that enough?

On the other side, many longtime residents of the city's once diverse neighborhoods are, not surprisingly, bitter. And for good reasons: gays are being priced out of the Castro, Latinos are being priced out of the Mission, African Americans are simply being physically displaced as their homes are torn down in Hunters Point to make room for condominiums. And where do art, music, and youth culture fit in this? Surely, many of the youthful techies enjoy the culture that the city has always bountifully provided, but just where are these artists supposed to live? And as for the city's many subcultures, like Buddhism, how exactly will Zen folks be able to continue to live anywhere near the San Francisco Zen Center when even a modest house rents for five to ten thousand dollars per month? The Zen Center itself may be able to survive, but its *sangha* (community) will be in exile along with other rent refugees. Worse yet, as Robert Reich comments in Pelosi's film, "San Francisco is a microcosm for what is happening not only in the United States, but all over the world."

Here is how it is happening. In his 2014 book *Average Is Over: Powering America Beyond the Age of the Great Stagnation*, Tyler Cowen offers the most complete description of and justification for an economy dominated by work with "intelligent machines," the economy for which San Francisco was the first "sacrifice zone" (as if it had been abandoned to mining or oil extraction). In the economy that Cowen envisions, there will be three classes: an upper 10 to 15 percent of high earners who will be working inside the digital economy; a middle class of workers (30–40 percent) who will provide services to the high earners (via an "entourage" workforce of chefs, massage therapists, life coaches, high-end bicycle mechanics, and so on), and then a near-bottomless caste of the irrelevant, for whom Cowen's best advice is "move to Texas where rents are cheap."

As an added benefit, the dispossessed will be "out of sight, and out of mind," where, as a Mafia don might put it, they'll be if not dead then "dead to me." Cowen's brand of libertarianism is the radical negation of Adam Smith's "impartial spectator," the moral agent who is supposed to watch over the human consequences of free markets. It is this observer who is supposed to say that it ought to be criminal to withhold essential public goods (shelter, food, medicine), and not a "best practice."[36]

But Cowen's libertarian dream is not without its ironies. Some of those who expected to prosper under tech's reign—who imagined thousands of affluent tech workers flowing into local stores, restaurants, and pubs—are now complaining that corporate campuses in San Francisco have themselves become gated communities within the greater gated community of the city. In July of 2018 two San Francisco supervisors introduced ordinances that would forbid free lunches in the cafeterias of new corporate office buildings. Why? According to Aaron Peskin, one of the ordinance's sponsors, "These tech companies have decided to leave their suburban campuses because their employees want to be in the city, and yet the irony is, they come to the city and are creating isolated, walled-off campuses . . . They're walled into their tech palaces."[37]

The human beings for whom global capital has ever less need are unwise to think that the system that has impoverished them can be made to reform itself. That is wishful thinking. It is also un-wise to think that through some great revolutionary action this sys-tem can be displaced. What is reasonable is to think: "I may not be needed, but I'm sure not alone." That's where we can find opportu-nity. In the process of pushing us away, techno-capitalism pushes us together.

In short, there is great undeveloped potential for democratic improvisation, for a strategic independence from national political and economic reality, *but*, nota bene, *first we must recognize this im-provisatory independence as what we want.* As I've said, we are not un-familiar with this independence, but there can and should be more of it. We need a *culture* of ever-larger tolerance for the impertinent and for those of independent will. Please note that I do not say that we need tolerance for impertinent individuals, even though we will most often see this impertinence in individuals. What I say is that we need tolerance for *cultures* of impertinence, which is, perhaps, to say nothing more than that we need cultures that are not founded upon inherited stupidities, because those stupidities are self-defeat-ing and they are killing and impoverishing us in very many ways.

If Freud had one hope, it was the rueful, plaintive, yet simple wish for a civilization that is less unhappy, less "discontented." It came to this for him: Human beings should be allowed to enjoy more pleasure without guilt and without punishment. Similarly, we as individuals and communities should be allowed more freedom for self-creation and self-development, without guilt and without punishment.

For Freud, it is a good thing that human instinctual drives are accomplished in culture and not in the woods. We don't merely want to survive, we want to thrive, we want to flourish, and we want to feel free to improvise socially, just as a jazz musician feels free to improvise musically.* The freedom to improvise does not mean dead-ending in one tribe or another, all organized through the fake democracy of the nation-state. It means, as every artist knows, thriving through our works, our curiosity, and our benevolence.

That should be our proper sense of *place*. This place is *proper* to us in the sense that it is most native to us, it is *truest* to who we are. It has been taken from us unfairly, and we ought to take back, or *claw back* (as restitution lawyers say) as much as we can. We have been cheated, so we should not be afraid to use a little claw, and maybe teeth, in our effort.

FINAL IMPROVISATION: A DEMONOLOGY

> *"Life on earth is inconceivable without trees. Forests create climate,*
> *climate influences peoples' character, and so on and so forth.*
> *There can be neither civilization nor happiness if forests crash down un-*
> *der the axe, if the climate is harsh and severe, if people*
> *are also harsh and severe.... What a terrible future!"*
> —Anton Chekhov, 1888

Most of us are aware of the way that capitalist economies impoverish and discard people, and we are increasingly aware of climate change: the tides rising over downtown; the deserts moving even more rapidly than the tides; the forests retreating ever further, ever

· ·

* There is a reason that the archetypal rock bands of the '60s, like the Grateful Dead, were free-form guitar improv bands led by guitar gods like Jerry Garcia, Fleetwood Mac's Peter Green, and Ten Years After's Alvin Lee. Reacting against the "canned music" of Top 40 radio, the trippy guitar solo led to *another world*.

more fragmented, due to deforestation, fire, and very busy beetles; and millions of climate refugees on the move, for whom the migrant caravan out of Honduras in the fall of 2018 was but a prelude. Millions more will join them in the next half-century, fleeing rising shorelines, annual once-in-a-century storms, and that new weather phenomenon "fire tornados." Mumbai, India, alone has 30 million people living more or less at sea level, and then there's the island of Manhattan . . . and the late great state of Florida.

What we don't know how to talk about, but that must figure in our thinking, are the humans among us who are substantially responsible for this situation, who are the walking equivalent of Buddhism's "hungry ghosts"—demons, let's call them. Perhaps it was of such people that Kant was thinking when he suggested that humans were "crooked timber out of which no straight thing was ever made." As overwhelming as natural catastrophe, there is human catastrophe, the catastrophe of character.

I recently worked my way through the twenty-six samurai movies that make up the series *Zatoichi, the Blind Swordsman*. The films were hugely popular in Japan in the '60s. Because of the sheer number of films made, they are of necessity formulaic: a blind yakuza master swordsman leaves the world of gangsters for a life on the road correcting injustice, protecting women, children, and the aged, and, in every climax, dueling with glamorous samurai "gun slingers"—all dressed in black, all with great hair—who lose their lives to Zatoichi's flashing cane sword. (Think Alan Ladd and Jack Palance in *Shane*.)

The villains are always the same: murderous yakuza bosses and corrupt government officials with their armies of sword-toting but expendable henchmen. (The henchmen lose their lives by the dozens, sliced up like the flies that Zatoichi kills in midflight.) These villains are indistinguishable one from the other. They are vain, mendacious, money hungry, and cruelly exploitive of women. Not unlike certain American presidents, one might observe.

I have a favorite line from Zatoichi that he repeats in several of his movies. Every once in a great while someone (usually a virtuous peasant) will selflessly aid the blind Zatoichi, after which he will observe, sotto voce, "I guess not everyone is a demon." If you did a head count (or body count) of the characters in these films, the people who put kindness ahead of self-interest would be only the tiniest of tiny minorities in a world full to the brim with demons. Even Zatoichi is part-demon: a not quite entirely reformed gambler and gangster who applies the *sake* liberally, cheats at dice (in qualified good conscience because he knows he's only cheating fellow demons), and frequently incites violence by deliberately offending thin-skinned gangsters.

It's a Saturday matinee version of the Buddhist idea that ours is the world of *dukkha*, a world of selfishness, cruelty, and endless suffering, or, as Zatoichi would put it, a world full of demons.

In the current political climate, Zatoichi's world and our own have a lot in common. Demons and demonizing are everywhere. Everyone outside of one's own immediate political circle is suspected of being a self-seeking liar whose victory would mean the failure of every human decency. Our opponents are people to whom a sword should be taken, or, as Trump put it, on whom the "second amendment people" should be loosed.

These political sects are mostly oblivious to their own faults and to their participation in a demonic world. From the college campus advocates of party line identity politics to the darkest of Trump's "dark state" conspiracy fanatics, all seem to be committed to a self-righteous sense of personal grievance and their own blamelessness. Each side casts the other in frighteningly reductive terms. Democrats are socialist baby killers, and the Republican base is stupid, violent, and bigoted.

What nobody seems to see in all of this is its bloodiness. None of our factions—whether democratic socialist, MAGA money-whore, or Tea Party zealot—is sufficiently self-critical to see that if they are to have what they claim to want, it will require violence. None of these groups has any intention of going passively into a world governed by the other side's notion of the common good. And why should they? Civic narcissists to the end, they're fixing the world!

During his 2016 campaign, Donald Trump repeatedly threatened civil unrest if he lost the presidential race because of a "rigged system." And then, as you know, there was Charlottesville. To a degree, our political reality resembles the Nazi Brown Shirts chasing communists around Alexanderplatz in 1933, and communists chasing them back in a hellish farce. We call them Proud Boys and Antifa now, in the streets of Portland or New York, but they belong in a wretched corner of Bosch's *Garden of Earthly Delights*, Donald Trump looming above them, like a deranged Thanksgiving parade balloon, urging them on.

This complicated if not utterly confused state of affairs should tell us at least one simple thing: what we are experiencing during the Trump presidency is not solely about Donald Trump. Is he like the gangster demons in Zatoichi movies? Sure. But the question for both Zatoichi and ourselves is, "What does it mean to be a demon in a world of demons?" It means that, whether homicidal yakuza boss or President of the United States, all are expressions of something much larger than themselves, and not in a good way. As a consequence, it is possible to say that Donald Trump does not exist, not even for himself. Even Trump has no idea who Trump is, as his constant retractions and his famously self-contradictory tweets show.

Donald Trump is a collective fantasy to which Donald Trump contributes. As Freud would have put it, he is a complex of ideas (in his case, incoherent ideas) to which psychic energy has been "cathected" (invested). For example, when you are in love, you focus an emotional charge on an object, the loved one. This object has nothing necessarily to do with a real person. Similarly, Trump partisans have cathected to an idol of their own unreasoned, jubilant, and angry creation.

Democrats are not innocent of this idolatry. They have cathected with the Clintons, Obama, Bernie Sanders, and now revitalized House Speaker Nancy Pelosi only to find their hope betrayed or disappointed by what is sadly familiar: the world made a secure place for capitalism, militarism, inequality, and environmental destruction. (Has there ever been an American president who was not also a war criminal or an arms dealer to war criminals? Even Obama learned to love the Predator drone.)

Through our dependence on political saviors, the bosses for our political gangs, we are—once again!—energetically conspiring in our own defeat. Because of this, our world will continue to be a welcome place for demons, ourselves among them, uncomfortably complicit, and we will have to find a way of living with that fact. It is the dilemma of Jean-Paul Sartre's *No Exit*: unable to confess or even understand our crimes, we are in a closed room tormenting each other with no idea how to leave. *"L'enfer, c'est les autres."* *Le démon, c'est moi!*

Lewis Thomas expressed this "demon's dilemma" memorably, poignantly, in *Late Night Thoughts on Listening to Mahler's Ninth Symphony* (1983). He describes listening to a "sane-seeming man," a civilian defense official, discuss ways for Americans to survive a nuclear war, and the advantages to us if only forty rather than eighty million people are killed. Then Thomas imagines what it must be like for a teenager to listen to such mad things knowing that there is no way to fix the madness:

> If I were sixteen or seventeen years old and had to listen to that, or read things like that, I would want to give up listening and reading. I would begin thinking up new kinds of sounds, different from any music heard before, and would be twisting and turning to rid myself of human language.[38]

Thomas died in 1993 and so never had to endure Donald Trump's paeans to our nuclear weapons arsenal, or President Putin's giddy announcement of the hypersonic nuclear missile "Avangard" in 2018,* but that only makes it easier for us to understand why Thomas's teenager considered ridding himself of human language

. . . .

* Commenting on Putin's speech, Kremlin analyst Gleb Pavlovsky said, "Only by telling everyone how he would destroy the world did the old man come alive."

in the hope that he could "exit" the world of the damned. But what I would like to call attention to is not Thomas's apparent fatalism but his call to think up "new kinds of sounds, different from any music heard before." If sixteen-year-olds are not to go mad, if any of us are not to go mad, we need to make the creation of these new sounds, new languages, and new cultures a very pressing duty.

PART
VI

LIVING IN PLACE

In a long essay, *The Harvard Black Rock Forest*, originally published in 1984 in *The New Yorker*, George W. S. Trow examined the history of New York's Black Rock Forest, a 3,800-acre site overlooking the Hudson River. In the early 20th century, after the forest had been reduced to the remains of small subsistence farms, it was bought by New York banker James Stillman. His son, Ernest Stillman, established the area as a demonstration forest in 1928 and bequeathed it to Harvard in 1940. Although the endowment Stillman left for the maintenance of the forest was more than sufficient to keep the forest project intact in perpetuity, the directors of Harvard began considering the sale of the land to Consolidated Edison in the early 1970s.* While Trow was deeply concerned about the fate of the particular (this particular forest and this particular instance of misplaced trust), he was equally interested in what those particulars had to say about the evolution of our *virtues*.

To describe this shift in our character, Trow imagined four kinds of "being-in-place" as a means of talking about virtue. For Trow, virtue cannot exist outside of place. Thus, people can be:

....

* Environmental groups sued Harvard to prevent the sale, and the forest is now managed by Black Rock Forest Consortium.

Mostly here: When people are "here," they are affected by and responsive to specific local conditions. This is the ethos of human settlements. This is people doing what they have to do to survive. It is "what works," but it is also rudimentary if not primitive.

Here and there: This is a situation in which a sense of place has been abstracted. Trow defined this as the "manner of the museum." The location of a museum usually has a relation to its collection, but the tendency is to remove the substance of the collection from any larger sense of place. Our national parks are in essence museums abstracted from their appropriate settings, settings that originally included people. The larger geographic context, where people now live, has been sacrificed to the interests of "resource extraction," as we dryly put it, industrial agriculture, and those enormous profit schemes we call cities.

Everywhere and nowhere: A strip mall or a condominium complex is nowhere and everywhere. It says nothing about a particular place, and yet it is, as we are too grimly aware, inescapably present in every American city and town. It is pure geographic alienation. It is only worse to realize that the "Ruling Order of Impersonal Forces" that will take your place (your forest, your community) has no interest in it as a place, and has no place of its own. It is drifting, hungry, and anonymous, but its activities are sadly familiar. It's what 7-11 did to that charming but dilapidated Victorian house on the corner. It's what Archer Daniels Midland does to family farms. It's what Amazon does to any- and everything that gets in its way.

The Harvard Black Rock Forest critiques our historical movement away from the virtue of "honorable men" (sorry) doing the "work of men" (so sorry) in a particular place, and toward the less-than-honorable work done by impersonal forces that are both nowhere and everywhere. Trow writes, "Clever men ally themselves with these forces, while idealistic men struggle to move certain valued things out of their way," perhaps to a museum where, obviously, no one lives. In Trow's judgment, that is not sufficient.

Nowhere and nowhere: In the present moment, we would have to add a new category to Trow's inventory of virtues: nowhere and nowhere. As the economy becomes ever more abstracted, the "everywhere/nowhere" shopping mall may become something we remember fondly. At least you could speed walk there on your lunch break, rather than having to dodge the delivery robots and electric scooters that have taken over the sidewalks. In the era of social media and smartphone addiction, an era that Trow did not live to see, we live in nowhere/nowhere. If it has a place at all, it is inside our skulls, but that sad place is capable only of "continuous partial attention." That is not a place; it is a socio- and psycho-pathology. And yet it is where we are now, and it is what we must confront if we are to survive and remain recognizably human.

Here and Everywhere: For Trow, virtue is found in none of these places. It is found in what Trow himself tried to practice—the virtue of being both "here" and "everywhere." People acting in a particular place with "clarity and sense" generate local virtues that become more general over time. Such virtues run "like a small channel throughout history." Ultimately, a commitment to these virtues becomes the spirit of a community.

At least that's how community is supposed to work. The poet C. D. Wright observes in a similar vein that the devaluation of virtue, of spirit, is a historical "retrenchment of human possibility":

> I believe that many members of "the tribe" [poets] . . . suffer
> the retrenchment of human possibilities, possibilities which
> for our thousand-and-one errors, we helped to create, which
> include the right and delight in choosing writing, even writ-
> ing poetry, over lawyering, banking, spying, advertising, pol-
> iticking, and other predatory arts, and that in helping to cre-
> ate these possibilities we simultaneously infected other areas of
> the population with similar yearnings.[39]

I hope that by now it is clear that what Wright is describing is the
logic of counterculture, world-making that invites, that says, "Really,
wouldn't you rather live here? Come this way! The view is great!"

Trow's work is important because he shows us how to inhabit, to
dwell within, to take on as if it were a garment, the tradition of
honorable work practiced locally. He performed this virtue for us
through this essay itself. (Isn't this what artists do when they try to
make the "here" of the Work the "everywhere" of the World?) He was
a literary man, a resident of that place we call the liberal arts, and it
was through his sense of style, his conceptual inventiveness, his acu-
ity as a reader, that he became both heroic and, strangely, lost.

Trow's virtues are lost on us because we are too much part of
the present moment, entrenched in a "predatory" world. We are the
proverbial lost souls marooned in a "nowhere" that is anything but
utopic. We live in our urban condo ghettos, our vinyl subdivisions,
or our McMansions, identical one to the other from California to
New Jersey. We wander like phantoms in our rationalized "trans-
portation systems," denied the comfort not only of place but also of
the warmth of other people, something that the advent of the electric car will not help with at all, never mind the bluer skies. Worst

of all, we have been taken up into the ether of the digital realm, our attention taken by our smartphones: all distraction, all the time. We find the source of our daily lives incomprehensible and yet, we suspect, ultimately trivial. The most we can claim is that this source has something to do with our precious "American lifestyle," something, we're told, that we should be willing to fight and kill for.

But from Trow's point of view, this appeal to "lifestyle" is just a way of saying that our lives are empty of authentic meaning and dignity. The problem and the tragedy is, of course, that Trow's critique cannot be heard in the midst of the noise made by our various wars to protect our sacred lifestyle against poorly understood things like "terror," or "crime," or "drugs," or, in Trump's crude reduction, the "immigrant," the dirty Other.

But even if there were a little less of the noise of our cold war civil war, we wouldn't understand Trow because we have so deeply internalized the logic of impersonal forces. Impersonal forces are not only "out there" acting on us; they are also "inside" of us (like Michel Foucault's "fascism within"). We can recognize this internalized force in all of the little "of courses" of our lives. Of course we need something called a job, money, cars, TVs, computers, gourmet gadgets, and the rest of it. Of course we hope the economy prospers. It's all about the economy, stupid. But be aware and beware: we cannot listen to these things to which we say "of course" and at the same time be able to hear Trow. In this context (which Trow called "the context of no context"), his thinking can only be something "interesting" that we hear about on NPR while commuting. It is just another media commodity, or, worse, the meme of the day. It is also something finally quite dead and irrelevant.

The point is this: it does not make sense to commit ourselves to economic and social processes (in education, work, health care, and housing) that are abstracted from the reality of *where* we are (nowhere, possessed by the Logic of Impersonal Forces), *who* we are (deluded and bloody-minded), and, most importantly, *where and who* we might prefer to be. George Trow's "here" is a place, but it is not just a place; to be a place at all it has to be first imagined, richly imagined for both good and bad. This forest and its history; this Harvard and its betrayal; and these virtues, these "fragments I have shored against my ruins," as T. S. Eliot put it. That's the wealth of imagination in which our self-styled "Resistance" has to move if it is not to become just another of history's bloody muckups.

This "wealth of imagination" already exists for us if we can find the intelligence to separate ourselves from our inherited stupidities in order to claim it (and I mean that "claim" to have the force of action, of revolt if not revolution). It is a tradition that not only tolerates but thrives on difference and on the cultivation of difference. It is a tradition of *educated* virtues taken from a school of thought that begins with the German and English Romantics and extends through the Concord transcendentalists, the British Arts and Crafts movement, and the varied Small is Beautiful countercultures of the mid-twentieth century led by Paul Goodman, E. F. Schumacher's *Study of Economics as if People Mattered*, and Christopher Alexander's "Pattern Language" school of architecture.

Alexander's "Pattern Language" school gave concrete direction to the New Urbanism philosophy of the 1960s—led by Lewis Mumford (*The City in History*, 1961) and others—that criticized the anomie of post-war suburban sprawl. Alexander's criticism of automobile-dependent community planning is sharp, and the technical details of Pattern Language have been widely influential, but what I find particularly inspiring and relevant in Alexander's work is its Romantic sensitivity to what humans need in their built environments. As he writes in *The Timeless Way of Building* (1979):

> [Consider] the Alhambra, some tiny gothic church, an old New England House, an Alpine hill village, an ancient Zen temple, a seat by a mountain stream, a courtyard filled with blue and yellow tiles among the earth. What is it they have in common? They are beautiful, ordered, harmonious—yes, all these things. But especially, and what strikes to the heart, they live. Each one of us wants to be able to bring a building or a part of a town to life like this. It is a fundamental human instinct, as much a part of our desire as the desire for children. It is, quite simply, the desire to make a part of nature, to complete a world which is already made of mountains, streams, snowdrops, and stones, with something made by us, as much a part of nature, and a part of our immediate surroundings. Each one of us has somewhere in his heart the dream to make a living world.[40]

School children should be made to memorize this passage and annually present it to the assembled student body, or be forbidden to advance to the next grade. Or have the principal read it over the intercom each morning in the place of the Pledge of Allegiance.

the Gettysburg Address,

Towards the end of the first volume of *The Man Without Qualities*, Robert Musil suggests that "we should live the history of ideas instead of the history of the world." In Musil's view, living the history of the world is circular and leads only to a repetition of the same mistakes made through violence and war at the expense of all living things. On the other hand, to live the history of ideas is open ended. The history of ideas is a dialogue or, better yet, a dialectic. It moves forward even if the world doesn't. Perched as we are at the edge (if not the end) of that history, Musil suggests that we live through what he calls "essayism," the "gliding logic of the soul," which opens upon "possibility." In ordinary terms, he's saying, essentially, "Instead of repeating the same deadly errors of official history—instead of stepping forward as a soldier, instead of getting on the train as a Good German, instead of saluting the flag as a patriot, instead of going to work, instead of nodding in assent when addressed through all of our shared stupidities—why don't we try something else, something that is more adequate to how we'd like to live?" As Musil writes:

> To pass through open doors, it is necessary to respect the fact that they have solid frames . . . But if there is a sense of reality . . . then there must also be something we can call a sense of possibility . . . the possible includes not only the fantasies of people with weak nerves but also the as yet unawakened intentions of God.

In writing this book—my own adventure in "essayism," my own attempt to create something living—I have been tempted at times to think that I should provide solutions. This is wrong. The critic's job is to bring readers to a point where they are free of certain familiar errors about what is real or true or necessary, and where they are free to make their own way forward through an openness to possibility. I don't know what you should do; I don't know what future countercultures should look like or how they should work. Humans are really good not at knowing but at learning, of being open to new ideas even if that involves a little permanent bewilderment. Needless to say, most of us are not looking for more ways to be bewildered: we are bewildered enough having to pick our way through this American life of tribalism with its hair on fire. But perhaps a little permanent social bewilderment means only this: *There is no best way to live and knowing that may be the best way to live.*

But I will say this: in the U.K. edition of my book about the atrophy of the American imagination, *The Middle Mind* (2004), I proposed a little mantra for "how to live" that comes as close as I can to a "solution," the basic purpose of which is to open out on possibility, on essaying. Perhaps that mantra is worth sharing again:

Misbehave: Refuse corporate life, consumption, work, militarism, nationalism, ideology, and social relations mediated only by money and technology. Refuse inherited stupidity. *you   first*

Make something beautiful: Make art outside of the dictates of the culture industry; make beautiful communities, homes, farms, landscapes, gardens; make beautiful tools, clothing, and furniture; make beautiful science, science not produced by "a morally irresponsible stooge in a science factory," as Norbert Wiener wrote in 1948; make morally woke science, as we might say.

Try to win: Create "families of choice" and communities of choice and then encourage others to do the same: Buddhist *sanghas*, food and housing co-ops, intentional communities of whatever kind. In Trow's language, winning is about making the "here" of freedom "everywhere."

This is perhaps heroic thinking, but, as the poet and memoirist May Sarton put it, "One must think like a hero to behave like a merely decent human being."

Wow!

PART
VII

CODA

We're living in a world that can't be fixed, and we need to live differently, but that doesn't mean that the world as presently arranged is going to go along with these conclusions. In fact it can be expected to resist in ways large and small. This resistance will begin with ideology, with telling us that, no, we *can* fix what's wrong with the world, and, no, we *don't* need to live differently. Bad as things may seem, there is time for self-correction.* Even worse, we will be told that any attempt on our part to live differently, to create countercultures, will not produce a better world; it will produce only familiar disasters. In short, we will be told that "countercultures always fail."

As an instance of this ideology, consider Maclain and Chapman Way's Netflix original *Wild Wild Country* (*WWC* hereafter), a larger-than-life documentary about Bhagwan Shree Rajneesh and his homemade paradise, Rajneeshpuram, in eastern Oregon in the early 1980s. I won't rehearse the scandalous history of the commune; it's enough for present purposes to say that it is full of deceit, betrayal, sex orgies (of course), assassination plots (surprisingly), bioterrorism

. . . .

* In other words, "Delusion will last until it is about to become fatal, at which point an onset of sanity is certain (John Kenneth Galbraith)."

(really surprisingly), and something close to civil war with the nativist Christians living down the road in the town of Antelope.

I'm also not much interested in the moral calculus concern-
ing heroes and villains that enflamed magazines, newspapers, and
websites upon the film's release in March of 2018. The media have
been particularly fascinated by the character of Ma Anand Sheela,
Bhagwan's secretary and Rajneeshpuram's primary administrator.
Was she "evil," as the prosecuting U.S. Attorney Robert Weaver
insisted, or was she just protecting her people and their right to
participate in a minority religion? Such questions are part of the
sensationalism that made the series so popular, but they aren't of
primary interest here.

According to the Way brothers, the film began with a happy
coincidence: they discovered three hundred hours of archival foot-
age about the Rajneesh commune at the Oregon Historical Society
while doing research for their first documentary, *The Battered
Bastards of Baseball*, a charming and uncontroversial film about
the Portland Mavericks, the last independent professional baseball
team. The Way brothers had no prior interest in New Age spiritual movements; they were merely looking for product, their "next
film." And Netflix, for its part, was looking for "content," something to help maintain the twenty million new streaming subscrib-
ers they gained in 2017. Baseball, Buddha: it was all the same to
them.

What is notable is the fact that in this archive the Way brothers
stumbled upon one of the first open conflicts in what would come
to be known as culture war. Seeing this distant origin of the current antagonism between "bicoastal elites" and the "Trump base"
is fascinating, like learning for the first time that the light that we

see from a star has been traveling toward us for thousands of years. Disappointingly, the Way brothers don't seem especially interested in how the Rajneesh conflict comments on the recent history of the culture wars.

Unfortunately, what they *are* interested in has more to do with "true crime" than social issues. For example, in the first episode of the series we are introduced to some of the good folk of Antelope. The surviving townsfolk are interviewed in their orderly and familiar homes, talking calmly and reasonably, full of good humor if not forgiveness. And yet their sense of once having been the victims of an outlandish group of religious crazies, perhaps a sex cult, remains strong. Their resentment for the "red people" (a reference to the colors in which Rajneesh's disciples dressed) is still palpable, and their sense that they should "keep Oregon Oregon" (that is, keep it white and Christian) is still vivid for them, as is their fear of becoming a minority "in our own country." Much to the Way brothers' credit, it is captivating to watch as rural friendliness passes over to xenophobia, and then back again to reasonable concern, all in the course of a sentence or two, rather like people who, in principle, want to be kind but who find that self-preservation makes it necessary to be cruel.

Following this introduction to local Oregonians, the Ways provide the first images of the sannyasins (devotees), the followers of Bhagwan. Ghostly figures dressed all in maroon wander in slow motion, aimless as zombies, down otherwise deserted streets. There is spooky, otherworldly music, perhaps meant to echo the soulless sound inside their heads. Members grin vacantly, and one plays the flute. From overhead, we see the beginnings of their massive "encampment," as the CIA might put it, as if it were a photograph of a secret Soviet missile site taken from a U2. *WWC* may be a Netflix Original, but this introduction feels more like the History channel's *Ancient Aliens*.

Moments later, the perception that there was something weird or demonic about the Rajneeshees is emphasized again through images of naked devotees writhing to heavy metal music. It's meditation as mosh pit, a Black Sabbath, real "worship this at your own risk" stuff. In other words, the visual rhetoric in these first scenes strongly suggests that the filmmakers share the panic of the citizens of Antelope: strange doings! As Bill Murray says in *Ghostbusters*, "Human sacrifice, dogs and cats living together—mass hysteria!"

Of course, the Way brothers do not endorse bigotry, and they later allow the blunt-spoken Ma Anand Sheela to name it for what it is. But why then, if they aren't xenophobic, would the Ways introduce us to the commune from such a morally canted angle? Are they trying to show us how the townsfolk *perceived* the Rajneeshees?

The answer is simpler than that: for the Way brothers, and implicitly Netflix, the weird intro is only a carny's come on for you-the-viewer. It's Dateline Oregon, a crime drama. The Way brothers are setting the narrative hook. The Rajneeshees are soon enough allowed to emerge from the alien haze in order to make their case, but, importantly, that case never wanders far from the scandals, the crimes, the lawsuits, and the bitter aftermath. It is only, if you will, what "Enquiring minds want to know."

Unfortunately, this approach means that a lot of worthy questions don't get asked. First, there is the question any decent police procedural should include: What did Bhagwan know about the criminal activities of his lieutenants and when did he know it? This one, you'd think, would be right in the Netflix wheelhouse. So in the course of the five days that the Ways spent talking with Sheela, why not ask?

There are other questions that don't get asked. Shouldn't any investigation of a religious group be curious about the group's beliefs? In other words, shouldn't the Ways have been curious about what exactly Bhagwan taught? He was obviously a very persuasive person. Thousands left their ordinary lives to follow him, and many thousands follow him still nearly thirty years after his death. It couldn't only have been that beguiling smile and those depthless brown eyes, could it? There must be something in all the books he wrote. Well, what was it?

There is only one moment in the film when we learn something from Bhagwan, or from anyone, about his theology (if that's the right word for it): he says that humans have two ways of dealing with sex. They can either repress sex or they can transform it. He was for transformation through creativity. He says, "Hence I teach my sannyasins to be creative. Create music, create poetry, create painting . . . Bring something new into existence and your sex will be fulfilled on a higher plane."

Obviously, that is not an outrageous teaching. It is far less outrageous than the attitude of the Christians of Antelope whose anxiety about a "sex cult" made them like medieval inquisitors of Cathar heretics, who were persecuted for sexual deviance because they preached celibacy. In fact, Bhagwan's eclectic teaching is nothing like the thinking of a sex cult: it is more like Freud's theory of libido transformed into creativity through sublimation. The Rajneesh was a syncretist who crudely joined Nietzsche and Freud to the Buddha and the *Bhagavad Gita* and then threw in a little Dale Carnegie for the fun of it (Bhagwan was adamantly, even aggressively, pro-capitalist). It would have been useful to have someone explain that fact in the film.

The Ways have frankly acknowledged that they are not "very well versed in spirituality." Worse yet, as Maclain Way explained in an interview with the movie review forum *MovieBoozer*, the brothers dislike documentaries "that have talking heads who have studied an issue for a really long time and have a PhD in something." The Way brothers prefer "storytelling" to an academic setting of context. Given their candor, it is perhaps small-minded to suggest that their lack of spiritual "verse" disqualifies them from making a film about a spiritual movement. After all, in the Information Age—dominated by Wikis, blog sites, and chat rooms, all watched over by smarter-than-thou trolls—my information is as good as anyone else's, even if I don't actually know anything.

Ironically, it appears that Bhagwan felt much like the Ways. It does not appear that there was any coherent intellectual authority behind Rajneeshism .beyond Rajneesh's personal charisma, nor were there any institutional traditions. The only proof for his authority was how one "felt," especially how one felt in his presence. Apparently, Bhagwan didn't need any PhDs either.

What this suggests is that both the filmmakers and their subject worked within George Trow's "context of no context." Both *WWC* and the religion it examines are ahistorical, and both lack an intellectual framework. Both are convinced that whatever they need can be summoned in the moment from their own idiosyncratic resources.

The downside of this approach is that the film comes almost

wholly from perspectives that are self-interested. Whether listening to members of the commune, neighbors, or lawyers, one has to listen to their stories "across the grain," that is, one has to listen skeptically and bring to the film the social, religious, and intellectual contexts that the film itself refuses to provide. That's a tall order for most people, which is why the judicious use of experts, people outside the fray, is a good thing in documentary filmmaking. Deprived of that, *WWC* devolves toward mere infotainment.

Another outrageously absent question is this: What was daily life like for the typical sannyasin? To judge from the comments of the commune members at the end of the film, even after all of the uproar and scandal, a lot of them were very sad when the commune closed and they had to move on. There were reasons for that sadness. As Milt Ritter, a cameraman for a local television station, said in an interview at the news website *Uproxx*:

Look at what the Rajneeshees did in just a few short years with this ranch that was completely depleted of everything. It was so overgrazed and in such poor, poor shape. They turned it into an oasis. They planted tens of thousands, maybe hundreds of thousands of saplings along the creeks. They replenished the riparian zones, and then they built that big dam and all those buildings. Some of them were not small buildings. It is amazing what they did. The organic farms, the meeting areas—it really is amazing what they did in such a short period of time.

The absence of any account of the daily experience of the commune caused Sunny Massad (formerly Ma Prem Sunshine) to complain to *Rolling Stone*, "I believed that he [Maclain Way] genuinely was going to do a story about the people that lived in the community—not just the few people who destroyed it."

If the leaders of the Rajneeshpuram were involved in a "criminal conspiracy," as federal attorneys proved in court, it plainly was not a conspiracy for everyone involved. Some of the people who lived there were guilty only of wanting Rajneeshism to be a real response to their own longing for something other than a brutal status quo that has only gotten more brutal since then (more debt, more soulless work, less education, more inequality).

The most articulate and persuasive spokesperson for those folks is Bhagwan's attorney, Philip J. Toelkes (Swami Prem Niren). His story is compelling: before the commune he was "burnt toast," a corporate lawyer, but in the commune he was "loved and accepted . . . for the first time." Toelkes is admirable not because of his loyalty to Bhagwan and his cult but *because of his loyalty to his own experience*. For the film's audience, Toelkes's testimony is dissonant: we feel that his loyalty to Rajneesh's cult of personality is mistaken, but we can't dismiss his claim that the community he discovered in the *puram* changed his life for the better.

This dissonance should have led to the biggest question, the opportune question that *WWC* seems willfully to ignore: "Why do people seek out cultures that are a negation of the culture into which they were born?" And this one: "Are such cultures viable alternatives for the future?" The dominant narrative in mainstream discourse is that the '60s are dead, the counterculture failed, and communes always end in disappointment and tragedy. Because *WWC* presents Rajneeshpuram primarily as a disaster, it only contributes to the widely received idea that communes shouldn't be attempted, are doomed to failure, are cons, and so forth.

This narrative presents itself as accepted wisdom even though it flies almost entirely in the face of the fact that every major aspect of the social turn that we know as the '60s counterculture is a living part of the present: anti-capitalism, feminism, gender equality, ethnic/racial equality, environmentalism, food and housing cooperatives, and—relevantly—alternative spiritual traditions, especially the ever-enlarging Western Buddhist community. San Francisco's Zen Center has had its share of scandals and challenges, but would a documentary similar to *WWC* do justice to its work and legacy? In spite of those scandals, Buddhist *sanghas*, meditation centers, and countercultures of whatever other stripe should continue to try to offer what Toelkes was so grateful to find at Rajneeshpuram: love, acceptance, and an alternative to the corporate sociality of money. As Slavoj Žižek has written of the Russian Revolution, echoing Samuel Beckett but in the spirit of Hegel, "Try again. Fail again. Fail better."

CODA CODA: WORK WITHOUT HOPE

In the *Bhagavad-Gita*, Krishna counsels Arjuna, who has been made hopeless by the idea that he has to fight his own cousins: "Work without hope of reward." Krishna's admonition means that Arjuna should be neither hopeful for some particular result for his effort, nor abandoned to the hopelessness that all effort is doomed.

Our situation is similar to Arjuna's. To think and to act in the ways I have encouraged here is to set oneself *counter* to things that demand our loyalty: the nation, perhaps our own families, and certainly some of the neighbors—that system of governmental, economic, social, and familial discipline that so often compels us to do the wrong thing, the destructive thing. This system demands our loyalty even when its demand is based on lies and stupidities, and even when it is clear that to deliver the loyalty that is demanded of us is to participate in unconscionable destruction.

To hope that this system can be fixed is delusional. But to be hopeless is to die to our own innermost feelings of concern for others and for a world of living things that seems every day a little closer to fatality. It is better, writes Dahr Jamail in his luminous book *The End of Ice* (2019), to be *hope-free*:

> Each time another scientific study is released showing yet another acceleration of the loss of ice atop the Arctic Ocean, or sea level rise projections are stepped up yet again, or news of another species that has gone extinct is announced, my heart breaks for what we have done and are doing to the planet. I grieve, yet this ongoing process has become more like peeling back the layers of an onion—there is always more work to do as the crisis we have created for ourselves continues to unfold. And somewhere along the line I surrendered my attachment to any results that might stem from my work. I am hope-free.[41]

Of course, we are not the first humans to have a vivid apocalyptic imagination, a strong "sense of an ending." In the 14th century there was the Black Death and the Hundred Years War that accompanied it, destroying somewhere between a third and a half of humanity from China through India, Europe, all the way north to Iceland. If a town lost only a third of its inhabitants to disease, it was fortunate. Many lost every soul, including the souls of dogs, cats, horses, and any other mammal in the unhappy environs. And then, as if there were a superfluity of sentient beings, tens of thousands of the survivors of the plague were destroyed in battle, in plundered towns, in cities under siege, or murdered on Europe's highways by marauding bands of unemployed soldiers.

Unimaginably bad as the 14th century certainly was, human cultural evolution gained from it, or so argues the historian Barbara Tuchman in her wondrous book *A Distant Mirror: the Calamitous 14th Century* (1978). She writes:

> Survivors of the plague, finding themselves neither destroyed nor improved, could discover no Divine purpose in the pain they had suffered. God's purposes were usually mysterious, but this scourge had been too terrible to be accepted without questioning. If a disaster of such magnitude, the most lethal ever known, was a mere wanton act of God or perhaps not God's work at all, then the absolutes of a fixed order were loosed from their moorings. Minds that opened to admit these questions could never again be shut. Once people envisioned the possibility of change in a fixed order, the end of an age of submission came in sight; the turn to individual conscience lay ahead. To that extent the Black Death may have been the unrecognized beginning of modern man.[42]

In short, because of plague and war Europe's peasants and merchants ceased to believe in the stories (the inherited stupidities of that time) that legitimized the authority of the clergy and the nobility. In time the merchant class would distinguish itself from the peasantry, take on the airs of the nobility, and become the new master class—capitalists—with a new set of stories to shore up their legitimacy: radical individualism, free markets, the work ethic, the necessity of money, and the nation-state under God.

These bourgeois myths are still the determinants of our own "age of submission," our own calamitous present. Frighteningly, our calamities could end up being even worse than the Plague and the Hundred Years War. Should the climate warm to five degrees above average, or should the world's narcissists-in-chief bring nuclear winter upon us, then that will be that, an end to evolution's short experiment with consciousness.

The good news is that the "absolutes" of our own "fixed order" can be loosed from their moorings, the impertinencies and improvisations of countercultures past and present have shown that. As Tuchman put it, "Minds that opened to admit these questions could never again be shut." And so, looking calamity in the face, our minds open, we are free to do something other than collaborate in our own destruction. We are freer to refuse to get on Musil's "train of history," freer to take up his "essayism," freer to create Christopher Alexander's "living world," and freer to take on a different way of living, all with counterculture's enduring and endearing purpose: a sustainable happiness achieved, as Wordsworth wrote, through "the calm existence that is mine when I am worthy of myself."

"The world is a den of thieves, and night is falling. Evil breaks its chains and runs through the world like a mad dog. The poison affects us all. No one escapes. Therefore let us be happy while we are happy. Let us be kind, generous, affectionate and good. It is necessary and not at all shameful to take pleasure in the little world."
—Ingmar Bergman, *Fanny and Alexander*

Acknowledgments

The idea of counterculture is so close to my heart, so large a part of who I am, that I feel I should thank not only those who have contributed to the writing of this book but also those who have helped me in the living of this life. So, in some rough approximation of chronological order: I am thankful for San Francisco (RIP), the Fillmore Auditorium, the Haight, Big Brother, Country Joe, Richard Brautigan, and the freaks and politicos of Berserkely. Those places and people provided a "portal of egress" from a culture that seemed to want to kill this suburban boy. I am thankful for teachers, especially John Barth and Gayatri Spivak, who deepened and enriched my voluntary internal exile. Thanks for the Fiction Collective—and within it: Ron Sukenick, Ray Federman, and Mark Leyner—which provided a DIY home for a clueless hippy pomo fictioneer. Thanks for my brothers-and-sisters-in-books, some of them departed: Donald Wolff, Geoffrey Green, Allen Dunn, Mary Papke, Douglas Messerli, John O'Brien, Charlie Harris, David Foster Wallace, Cheston Knapp, and Rikki Ducornet. Thanks as always for editors, for Roger Hodge, Gideon Weil, Peter Richardson, Kelly Burdick, and, in the present case, Ryan Harrington—I doubt that I would ever have written a decent book without y'all. And thanks for those students who became life companions: Ben Slotky, A. D. Jameson, and Martin Riker.

But mostly, mostly thanks for my family and the sustaining love in our "little world": my wife Georganne Rundblad, my daughter Megan White, my son-in-law Jason Thomas, and the rest of our happily bewildered "fambly"—without them I would have lacked courage. Thanks no less for our family of choice, the Africanos, in our "compound," our rehabbed Soldiers and Sailors Orphanage in, of all places, a Midwestern town called Normal.

To have such reasons for gratitude is itself a reason to be grateful.

As for this book: it wouldn't have happened without my conversations with Dahr Jamail while hiking in the Olympic Mountains. Thanks Dahr.

Portions of this book appeared in different form in *Salon, In These Times,* and *Tricycle* magazines, and in the literary blog sites *Big Other* and *Moby Lives.*

Endnotes

INTRODUCTION

1   Paul Goodman, *Growing Up Absurd: Problems of Youth in the Organized System* (New York Review Books, 2012), 35.

PART I

2   Quoted in Maria Paradia, "Forgetting Sufferers . . ." *Occupy.com*, December 2, 2017.

3   Peter Buffett, "The Charitable-Industrial Complex," *The New York Times*, July 26, 2013.

4   Slavoj Žižek, *Trouble in Paradise: From the End of History to the End of Capitalism* (Melville House, 2017), 166.

5   Julie Creswell, "Young and In Love . . . with Lipstick and Eyeliner," *The New York Times*, November 22, 2017.

6   Antonio Negri and Michael Hardt, *Assembly* (Oxford University Press, 2017), 101.

PART II

7   Ed Pilkington, "A journey through a land of extreme poverty: welcome to America," *The Guardian*, December 15, 2017.

8   E. W., "Democracy in America," *The Economist*, February 22, 2016.

9   Don Lee, "Americans are moving house much less," *The Los Angeles Times*, December 28, 2017.

10 Charles Murray, *Coming Apart: The State of White America 1960-2012* (Crown Forum, 2012).

11   Michael Hobbes, "Why Millennials are facing the scariest financial future of any generation since the Great Depression," *Highline, HuffPost,* December 2017.

12   Christopher Flavelle, "Florida's real-estate reckoning could be closer than you think," *Bloomberg News,* December 29, 2017.

13   Orrin Pilkey, *Sea Level Rise: the Slow Tsunami on America's Shores,* (Duke University Press, 2019).

14   Oliver Milman, "We're Moving to Higher Ground: America's Era of Climate Mass Migration is Here," *The Guardian,* September 24, 2018.

Part III

15   Nancy Fraser, "From Progressive Neo-liberalism to Trump—and Beyond," *American Affairs,* Vol. I, Number 4.

16   Anthony Tomassini, "Andrew Norman's 'Split,' a Teeming Premiere From the New York Philharmonic," *The New York Times,* December 11, 2015.

17   William Rivers Pitt, "Why I hate Michael Wolff's new Trump book," *Truthout,* January 10, 2018.

18   Timothy Egan, "God, Don't Save the King," *The New York Times,* March 2, 2018.

19   Christopher Lebron, "*Black Panther* is Not the Movie We Deserve," *Boston Review,* February 17, 2018.

20   Osha Neumann, "A White Guy Watches *The Black Panther,*" *CounterPunch,* February 23, 2018.

21   David Brooks, "The Art of Thinking Well," *The New York Times,* October 10, 2017.

22   George Monbiot, "The Power of Stories: Why We Need More than Facts to Win," *Truthout,* October 19, 2017.

Part IV

23   Ed Pilkington, "Feel the love, feel the hate—my week in the cauldron of Trump's wild rallies," *The Guardian,* November 1, 2018.

24 Kevin Baker, "Political Party Meltdown," *The New York Times*, December 19, 2015.

25 Nathan Schneider, *Everything For Everyone: The Radical Tradition That is Shaping the Next Economy* (Bold Type Books, 2018), 5.

26 Christopher Alexander, *A Pattern Language: Towns, Buildings, Construction* (Oxford University Press, 1977), 13.

27 Ibid, 44.

28 Lewis Thomas, *Late Night Thoughts on Listening to Mahler's Ninth Symphony* (Viking Press, 1983), 161.

Part V

29 Kate Taylor, "Fast Food CEO Says He's Investing in Machines," *Business Insider*, March 16, 2016.

30 Andy Beckett, "How to Spend It: the Shopping List for the 1%," *The Guardian*, July 19, 2018.

31 Michael J. de la Merced and Nathaniel Popper, "JPMorgan Chase Moves to Be First Big U.S. Bank With Its Own Cryptocurrency," *The New York Times*, February 14, 2019.

32 Nellie Bowles, "The Dawn of a Crypto Utopia?" *The New York Times*, February 4, 2018.

33 Douglas Rushkoff, "Survival of the Richest," *Medium*, July 5, 2018.

34 Rosa de Ferari, "The Silent Massacre: Chronic Kidney Disease in Central American Sugarcane Workers," *Panoramas*, University of Pittsburgh, November 14, 2017.

35 Jean Baudrillard, *America* (Verso, 2010), 112–113.

36 Tyler Cowen, *Average is Over* (Plume, 2013).

37 Nellie Bowles, "San Francisco Officials to Tech Workers: Buy Your Lunch," *The New York Times*, July 31, 2018.

38 Lewis Thomas, *Late Night*, 168.

PART VI

39   C. D. Wright, *Cooling Time* (Copper Canyon, 2005), 10.

40   Christopher Alexander, *The Timeless Way of Building* (Oxford University Press, 1979), 8.

PART VII

41   Dahr Jamail, *The End of Ice: Bearing Witness and Finding Meaning in the Path of Climate Disruption* (The New Press, 2019), 218–219.

42   Barbara Tuchman, *A Distant Mirror: the Calamitous 14ᵗʰ Century* (Alfred A. Knopf, 1978), 123.